Dharma and Communalism

Dharma and Communalism

Narendra Mohan

PRABHAT PRAKASHAN

Published by
PRABHAT PRAKASHAN PVT. LTD.
4/19 Asaf Ali Road,
New Delhi-110 002 (INDIA)
e-mail: prabhatbooks@gmail.com

ISBN 978-93-90366-56-9
***DHARMA* AND COMMUNALISM**
by Shri Narendra Mohan

Edition
First, 2022

Price
₹ 500.00 (Rupees Five Hundred only)

Cover layout
Shri Avadhesh Rajput

Printed at
R-Tech Offset Printers, Delhi

To
Respected Gurudev
Swami Ram

Foreword

'The memory of the past is called love; and love should remain silent'–this has continued to be a common saying for ages; but this could never be a reality. I have known Narendra Mohan, the author of this book, since his childhood. Since those days, he has been extraordinarily brilliant and fearless. He has even gone through tortures behind the bars.

In this book, he has expressed his emotions and sentiments on the subjects like Dharma, society and country covering all aspects of life. 'Dharma' is the word that has the greatest influence on common and universally recognised moral values. It is an irony that 'Dharma', which is eternal, which is never transient and which is worth embracing, is itself being used to spread most of the misconceptions and discords. The same India, which has propagated the message of ***Vasudhaiva Kutumbakam i.e. 'the world is one family', is today so ensnared by the materialistic glamour of the West that it is not able to find a way to come out of the same.***

What could be a better service to humanity than an attempt to establish common and universally recognised moral values, ignoring exposition of Dharma based on philosophical interpretation of hearsays and recollections? There are many aspects common to all religions of the world; it is the need of the hour to propagate and promote those common aspects everywhere. Mankind is currently blessed with a great opportunity with easy accessibility to excellent and effective modes of communication and information exchange on account of scientific developments. If only that opportunity is exploited properly to establish an order of goodwill and cooperation in the world, our earth may get rid of the problems and we may have peace and prosperity all around.

Time and again, persons of great repute from all religions have offered their suggestions and attempted to guide the world for eradication of the ills of contemporary societies. Most of their advices are common in nature, 'compassion' or 'kindness' being the most important of all. Truthfulness is espoused in all religions with the same intensity. Furthermore, even importance given to virtues like righteousness, humility, non-violence, philanthropy (sacrificing surplus resources for use of others), proper care for slaves and servants and refraining oneself from hatred, animosity, anger, theft and self-praise are found in all religions in equal measure. In addition to this, there are references in history to such religious rulers who set out rules and regulations for propagation and promotion of the same moral values and prescribed punishments for not abiding by the same. Inscriptions of Gautama Buddha, Mahavira and Ashoka are still available as testimony to the same.

20 December, 1995
Himalaya Sansthan
Jolly Grant, Dehradun

—Swami Ram

Author's Note

It is a matter of great concern that an atmosphere of misconception is getting created with the word *'Dharma'* and its real meaning is misterpreted. That too in a country where Dharma has long been considered as a synonym for righteousness. Ideally, there should have been sincere efforts to find a suitable solution to this problem. Instead, we Indians are also getting entrapped into the same vicious circle that has been created by Western ideologues by propagating Dharma as a synonym of 'Religion'. The question here is - can this misconception be eliminated? Definitely this misconception can be eliminated, with us Indians distancing ourselves from the Western influenced philosophy. According to Indian philosophy, Dharma is eternal. Hence, when it is interpreted in totality, it becomes synonymous to the Supreme Being and hence indescribable. The philosophy relating to the level below that totality, the philosophy of temporal dimensions, interprets Dharma in terms of karma based on duty or based on feasibility. And it is here that Dharma becomes synonymous to righteousness. Indian scholars have also recognised a different eternal facet of Dharma. Accordingly, Dharma is the essentiality that actually defines the materialisation of any matter. Indian philosophy has also presented to the world the idea that every organic and inorganic matter has its own domain and every domain has its own Dharma. That very Dharma becomes the eternal character of that domain. Thus, two different matters would not have same Dharma, just as Dharma of water is different from the Dharma of fire. The Dharma of water is to flow and Dharma of fire is to burn and to cause to burn. Apart from this, another interpretation has also been presented that suggests that the goal of Dharma should always be welfare for all. However, Western philosophy has linked Dharma to temporal morality, social obligations or to a Supreme Being. This being can be pleased, can be angered, is the almighty and creator and lives somewhere beyond this world. The West has always perceived Dharma with an extroverted thinking whereas India has attempted to understand Dharma with an introspective thinking. For Indian scholars, Dharma is neither an ideology, nor a traditional philosophy, nor thinking; it also does not have any direct linkage to the social morality that has been detailed in 'Holy Scriptures'. Indian philosophy acknowledges that Dharma is a conscious perception of the supreme one that transforms the inner self and also imparts divineness.

The contradictions and differences in opinion that exist between Indian and Western thinking have generated misconceptions with Dharma, and malicious aspersions are being cast on it. An attempt has been made in this book to present some thoughts that may help in confronting those misconceptions and aspersions. No claim has been made that the definition of Dharma that has been presented in this book is the best one; such a claim cannot even be made. An attempt has just been made here to re-enunciate the long-established Indian philosophy and the way it has been traditionally understood. There is nothing new in this book. Materialists of current generation may or may not understand Dharma the way Indian scholars have understood. It is however still believed that Dharma would continue to exist. Dharma may or may not get felt or realised, but it is a fact that we Indians perceive Dharma as synonymous to truth and this is not a shifting ideology. Eternal Dharma, which is also referred to as perennial truth, cannot be used for self-seeking aggrandisement. It cannot be linked to narrow-mindedness, intolerance or prejudice; nor can it be presented as a set of directives. Dharma is perpetual, perennial, and universal, available to every living being - just as sunlight reaches everybody without discrimination. Sunlight however is accessible only to those who really want to see it. If somebody keeps his eyes shut deliberately or because of ignorance, sunlight would not be accessible to him.

A vicious situation has developed on account of treating Dharma as synonymous to 'Religion'. The vehement support it has received from the nexus of Western propaganda and politics have not only made Indians to dither but also to almost stop accepting Dharma as synonymous to truth. This is a matter of grave concern. Fortunately, the architects of the Constitution of India recognised Dharma as the eternal and perennial truth. They have adopted a goal-oriented *mahavakya* (great pronouncement) for the parliament-'धर्मचक्र प्रवर्तनाय' (*'Dharmachakra pravartanaya'*). Similarly, the *mahavakya* adopted for judiciary is - 'धर्मो रक्षति रक्षितः' (*'dharmo rakshati rakshitah'*). Still, this word 'Dharma' is being disgraced in present times in our country and all this is happening because of political self-seeking, deviousness and ignorance. Another reason for this is also that influence of Western culture on the national psyche is of late increasing at a fast pace. An attempt has been made in this book to present different aspects of Dharma and related issues. It is the aim of this book to encourage restoration of proper thinking in respect of Dharma in this country. The situation is currently in a very bad shape due to commercialisation of Dharma, further complicated with the involvement of politics. A resolution to this situation may be found only if Dharma is defined appropriately and people embrace the same in their way of life. This requires a definite resolve. If Indians in general do not make that resolve, future generations may get deprived of those great concepts of Dharma. Those that are based on truth, righteousness and duty and that do not have any place for selfishness, narrow-mindedness, intolerance and exploitation. Not only that, the Indian psyche would fail to withstand the Western cultural assault effectively with a fallacious understanding of Dharma.

Dharma has been publicised all around the world as something else, not a science. With the same logic, it is also being propagated that Dharma has nothing to do with rationality and hence would always be accompanied by hypocrisy and superstition. On the other hand, science is completely logical and rational. The philosophy of treating Dharma and science as opposite to each other is the consequence of atheism-oriented thinking. This believes neither in Chaitya doctrine nor in Vaisya doctrine nor in Paramatma, the Supreme Being. The number of such people who prefer to live only at the level of body, mind and intellect is currently on the rise. These are the people who are especially responsible for depriving Dharma of (the word 'of' is to be added) its real status. These are the people who have contributed the most in promoting misinterpretation of the meaning of Dharma. In this regard, the blame also falls on the class of people who occupy so-called high religious positions and treat themselves as priests. Ordinary priests of today have given preference to their self-interest and self-importance over rationality. How and when are humans going to get rid of the growing influence of self-interest, egoism and orthodoxy, which have overtaken rationality and conscious reasoning? This is an important question of this time. There is also one more important question - is there any solution to the evil designs attempting to divide humanity into multiple segments? Definitely, Western culture and modern spiritual philosophy are not able to find answers to these questions. Instead, they are further complicating the situation. The irony is that, the existing Indian philosophy is also gradually falling prey to the cultural colonialism of the West. Today's India does not appear to have the capability to withstand this Western cultural invasion.

Indian sages and philosophers had, after vigorous (rigorous – is more apt) brainstorming on Dharma, arrived at the conclusion that Dharma was a radical internal change primarily aimed towards a transformation of one's inner-self by experience and realisation such that he or she is integrated perfectly not only with the living world but also with Mother Nature. According to these Indian scholars, Dharma is an experience - of omnipresent divinity, of Param Chaitanya and of supreme existence. The thought process of the West in respect of Dharma was based on a sense of fear. The philosophy of 'Religion' or 'Mazahab' is community focused. That is filled with self-interest. All the concepts developed in the West in the name of 'Religion' or 'Mazahab' were linked to either a specific period in the past or a great person or a specific book. Indian philosophers did not link Dharma to either a book or an individual.

The Indian philosophy exhorts performing one's duties while

residing within the eternal and welfare-oriented consciousness of Dharma. Every individual is a part of the whole, while really being whole himself. For the West, this Indian observation may be quite mysterious as Western philosophy is extroversive. Whatever Indian philosophers have achieved has been accomplished by diving into introverted consciousness. As per Indian thinking, Dharma has to be experienced and Dharma can be experienced only if we believe in the adage 'आत्मन: प्रतिकूलानि, परेषां न समाचरेत्', the only essence of Dharma. This book also explores the thoughts that may help to find out and understand the essence of Dharma.

In this book, I have also included some of my articles, with due modifications, which I had written for my weekly column '*Vichar Pravah*' on the issues of Dharma and communalism. These articles have been deliberated and discussed by the intellectual community from time to time.

—Narendra Mohan

Contents

1

The Mystery of Dharma

The word that has been misused the most by human beings is 'Dharma'. There has been a long tradition of misuse of this word and nobody knows when humans would stop it or whether at all they would stop it. This word that has been interpreted arbitrarily the most is also the word 'Dharma'. There is a lot of discord on the actual meaning of this word 'Dharma'. Similarly, the word that has been used the most for serving personal interest is also 'Dharma'. Coincidentally, this is also an indisputable truth that humans have their strongest faith in this very single word.

Dharma encompasses all aspects of a human being. And 'Dharma' is such a convoluted word in itself that there are now disputes even over the capacity of mankind to uncover all its mysteries. Despite being the greatest mystery, human beings have the most respect and devotion for Dharma only. This devotion towards it sometimes develops into superstition and obsession. This, to such an extent that a person becomes ready to sacrifice not only his life but also his very existence to safeguard what he believes to be Dharma. On the one side, humans have used this word to accomplish maximum creative achievements, to evolve themselves and to unveil the greatest values of humanity. On the other side, they have also shed maximum blood in the guise of the same word. Most of the wars, most of the killings, maximum exploitation and extreme victimisation have all happened in the name of 'Dharma'. The kinds of tyranny and barbarity that humans have indulged in using the shield of 'Dharma' have not been used by them even to save their own lives. All the hypocrisy of mankind and all the superstitions are related to 'Dharma' only, though the same 'Dharma' has been the source of their greatest achievements. Why at all does this paradox exist in respect of 'Dharma'? There is a need to explore and understand the same.

Indian sages have considered 'Dharma' to be perpetual and eternal. They always believed in the maxim 'Dharma is the truth and truth is the Dharma'. This had been the belief of all those visionaries of truth who incarnated themselves sometime as Vedic seers, as Mahatma Buddha, as Mahavira, as Jesus Christ, as Muhammad Sahab and as Mahatma Gandhi. The main point is that the world still holds in high esteem the accomplishments of those who entered the domain of Dharma, made attempts to seek and understand its real character and dedicated themselves to the same with full devotion. Only those who treated their lives as research laboratories to get a clear perception of Dharma could actually have a glimpse of its perpetuity. Those who only believed the hearsays in the guise of Dharma turned out to be sectarian. And when their sectarianism reached the point of hysteria, they became fanatics and criminals.

'Dharma' is a realisation that one has to experience on his own. 'Dharma' is a transformation that takes place within a person only when he applies his entire life force and intel lectual power with intense inquisitiveness.

'Dharma' is a realisation that one has to experience on his own. 'Dharma' is a transformation that takes place within a person only when he applies his entire life force and intellectual power with intense inquisitiveness to explore and research it. Each and every particle in this world is guided by Dharma. Dharma exists in every molecule. The entire operation of Mother Nature, its whole arrangement is controlled by and steeped in Dharma. If Dharma disappears from the system of our Mother Nature even for a moment, everything would disintegrate and get shattered and destroyed. And moreover, not only the earth but also the structure of the entire universe would collapse. This also is amazing to think that if a power does exist in this universe or even beyond this universe, that power also would be based on some Dharma or, if we may say so, on some definite regulations. Development and operation of this creation is possible only by some pre-determined eternal arrangement.

This very eternal arrangement of Dharma is the basis of existence of this creation. Misuse or misinterpretation of Dharma results in narrow-mindedness, sectarianism and perversity. Dharma in its perverse form becomes a reason even for battle and barbarism; but when used in its true form, i.e. if imbibed in one's way of life, it is instrumental in developing creativity, amity and cordiality.

When Dharma gets oriented towards realisation and becomes the bearer of life energy, it starts resonating each and every element of the soul and this results in generation of new dimensions for creation, transcendence and common good. This regime of Dharma, this mystery cannot be expressed in words. Words, though, may surely help in getting a partial glimpse of the same. When the structure of the entire universe is dependent on Dharma, how can the authority of the Whole, the Supreme Being be separated from Dharma? It's only Dharma that embraces truth; if there were nobody to possess truth, it would become abstract and formless. In order to provide truth a real form, there has to be some arrangement to help create that form. That very arrangement is called '*Dharma*'. The significance of 'Dharma' cannot be described in books. Even the greatest scriptures would be incomplete and insufficient and would look insignificant in front of actual realisation.

When Dharma gets oriented towards realisation and becomes the bearer of life energy, it starts resonating each and every element of the soul and this results in generation of new dimensions for creation, transcendence.

Dharma is not only a realisation but also a kind of experience that is eternal and perpetual which means that it is kept afloat through *karma*. Dharma has a connection with *karma*. Dharma is not just a philosophical speculation; it is an eternal truth. Dharma cannot be constrained by definitions. Its real form cannot be realised and understood by using it as a subject for debate or discussion. If this word is to be realised and understood, if this has to be experienced and if the layers of its mysteries have to be unfolded, the essence of 'Dharma' would need to be brought into the domains of *karma* and experience.

An insight of the real power of 'Dharma' can be had only through the means of *karma*. Karma only can establish the arrangement where 'Dharma' and hypocrisy may be differentiated. 'Dharma' would be treated as hypocrisy if it cannot be moulded into *karma*. In the context of Dharma, karma can be divided into multiple forms. In one of its forms, *karma* is used to achieve something; there is also another form that is not affected by any desire. In the second form of *karma*, the performer has neither a desire nor an aspiration of his own. In this form, *karma* becomes a character of the performer and the same is treated as an identification of his existence. This moulding of *karma* as character is a transformation that not only nurtures Dharma the most but also helps brighten its personality. In the absence of a performer, both Dharma and karma lose existence and they cannot be experienced. The moment a performer comes into play, his karma that symbolises his existence can be treated as his fundamental character. That very fundamental character is the primary Dharma of the performer. Just like inflammability is the Dharma as well as the character of fire, the basic character of a substance or performer cannot be changed with the help of desire or aspiration. Any change in the basic characters of the substance and performer would bring an end to their very existence. Till the time the sun is providing light and till the time water is making things wet, it can be said that the existence of sun and water are just following their 'Rit Dharma'. It can be hence concluded that all the substances and components that are available in this Creation, do have at least some of their own characters. The real character of a substance is also its real Dharma. In a way, we may say that Dharma is only the one that can be tested against the criteria of character. Anything that cannot be tested against the criteria of character cannot be called real Dharma. Thus, Dharma must find a place in the laboratory of the world in the form of 'character' and 'karma'; then only that would be called 'Rit Dharma'. It would not be righteous to call anything Dharma if the same cannot be tested in the laboratory of life and scrutinised with

An insight of the real power of 'Dharma' can be had only through the means of karma. Karma only can establish the arrangement where 'Dharma' and hypocrisy may be differentiated.

our rationality and intelligence. Superstition and ignorance cannot be treated as Dharma. Blind faith and hypocrisy also cannot be accepted as Dharma. The real Dharma is actually just the opposite to superstition and blind faith.

This is required to be understood clearly that Dharma gets developed in a human being out of his curiosity. Whatever may be the strength of a substance or its character, this is natural for a human being to get attracted towards the same. A person would certainly have some interest or curiosity for a substance that comes into contact with him. Ultimately, that curiosity only pushes him to the path of Dharma and guides him towards contemplation, cogitation and deliberation. Curiosity does not have any conflict with Dharma; instead it is helpful in accomplishing Dharma. Here, accomplishing Dharma does not mean something like picking an object already lying in a cupboard. Dharma is available in this world only as character or karma. The existence of every entity depends on its Dharma i.e. basic character of that entity.

A person would certainly have some interest or curiosity for a substance that comes into contact with him. Ultimately, that curiosity only pushes him to the path of Dharma and guides him towards contemplation.

To learn about the existence of Dharma or to understand its mysteries, one has to get into the domain of experience and realisation. Those who do not have the capability to get into that profoundness or those who get scared of darkness or get afraid of the unknown cannot understand the mysteries of Dharma. Dharma, thus, makes us courageous and hence, those who are the real followers of Dharma are always ready for self-sacrifice to protect their values. This is the reason that, for a real follower of Dharma, there is no existence of ego for self. He actually delves so deep to find out and understand the meaning of Dharma that his own existence merges completely with enormousness of Dharma; in a way, he loses his own existence. Just like, when a drop of water proceeds to explore the ocean, it drops into the ocean and itself becomes the ocean; the existence of that drop is lost. Thus, the real aspiration of a loyal follower of Dharma is to merge with the Whole and attain the same. No words can express the feeling of that merger with the Whole.

A question may be raised in this regard - can the realisation of 'Dharma' be achieved through karma or can the mysteries of Dharma be uncovered by any of our actions? In a sense, this may be possible, though, in another sense, this may not be possible. Where it is possible, Dharma originates when the complexion of Param Chaitanya i.e. all-pervading power is expressed in infinite forms; in reality, this Param Chaitanya is the Supreme One and is non-dual. But, why this Supreme Being that is non-dual, appears to us as dual and why the same takes infinite forms? A human being does not have the capacity to explain this. Those who have the knowledge of spiritual philosophy are silent on this matter; rather, they should definitely remain silent. Only that all-pervading power i.e. Param Chaitanya has the capacity to answer this question. We recognise this Chaitanya as Param Bramha. This Chaitanya also must be having some character. That character is the Dharma for that Chaitanya. When we define Dharma at the level of the all-pervading power, it does not have any connection with karma; Dharma can be perceived only as character. This Param Bramha, by its own nature, expresses itself through its existence for the purpose of fun and enjoyment. This manifestation of Param Bramha is timeless and ubiquitous and is so colossal that nobody would be ever able to perceive it entirely. Of course, those who delve deep into the same all the way, may sometimes get a fleeting glimpse of the same but that is generally incomplete and vague. This may be explained with an analogy. A wave cannot perceive the ocean in its entirety. Same is the limit for the thought process of a human being. When a wave treats itself as a wave or when that wave assumes itself to be following the nature of a wave, that wave is actually constrained by a Dharma and it becomes its Dharma to move up, move down, move up again and move down again, get merged sometime, become silent some other time, assume a frightening shape

A question may be raised in this regard- can the realisation of 'Dharma' be achieved through karma or can the mysteries of Dharma be uncovered by any of our actions? In a sense, this may be possible, though, in another sense.

sometime, connect with other waves some other time etc. In this ocean of Chaitanya i.e. consciousness, a human being has the same status as that of a wave in an ocean. The human being is an amusement for Chaitanya and also a part of Chaitanya. This amusement of Chaitanya may be perceived as its 'Rit Dharma'.

The mystery of 'Dharma' becomes more mysterious and complicated when a person assumes himself to be a performer as well as consumer. Something like a wave of ocean ignorantly treating itself to be separate from the ocean and assuming itself to be a separate existence. There is neither a wave in the ocean nor an existence separate from the ocean; that means there is no performer and also there is no consumer. There is only one undivided infinity that is beyond words, beyond experience and beyond realisation. Nobody knows what lies within that undivided infinity. Hence, nobody would also know what really the 'Dharma' of that undivided infinity is. Who would uncover the mystery of 'Dharma' of that infinity and who would understand the same? If at all anybody like that would be there, that would be none other than the infinity itself. That infinity is undivided and complete and there cannot be anything separate from the same.

The mystery of 'Dharma' becomes more mysterious and complicated when a person assumes himself to be a performer as well as consumer. Something like a wave of ocean ignorantly treating itself to be separate from the ocean.

The West considered morality as 'Dharma' and imposed a number of prescriptions and instructions on an individual. India did not connect morality to Dharma directly. Indian philosophers have believed that morality and Dharma have separate paths. Those who treat morality as Dharma maintain that whatever is not moral, not true and not beneficial for the society must be discarded and that which is true, correct and beneficial for all must be brought in. Indian philosophy suggests living in the realisation of eternal consciousness of the Supreme Being and striving to enter into the consciousness of eternal Supreme Soul. As per Indian philosophy, Dharma actually symbolises perpetual awareness of the ubiquitous Supreme Soul. It is considered that Dharma is such a state of consciousness or such a realisation where entry of falsehood is not possible. Even entry of perversion, darkness and impurity would not be possible in such a state of enlightenment. Hence, a righteous person has to just awaken from the state of his ignorance. He just needs to be aware of his own perpetually enlightened soul. Once a person gets enlightened with the brilliance of his own soul, the entire darkness, entire perversion, ignorance and immorality disappears by themselves.

□

2

Controversy on Dharma

Possibly this question might be arising right from the time human beings understood the existence of 'Dharma'- who would affirm what constitutes 'Dharma' and what constitutes 'Adharma'? What would be the criteria to validate 'Dharma' and 'Adharma'? Can we constrain 'Dharma' by those interpretations only that are detailed in religious scriptures? Would it be possible to decide on the affirmation based on the definitions provided by those scriptures? If we treat the definitions provided by the scriptures as criteria, which one of the definitions would we consider as the most important? Each of the scriptures cannot be considered as a criterion and we will need to bestow special importance to one of them only. And this becomes the starting point for disputes and controversies. Should we give importance to Vedic verses or Upanishads, to 'Dhammapada' of Mahatma Buddha or 'Jain Sutras' of Mahavira, to 'ayats' of Quran Sharif or inferences of Bible or to some other religious scripture? Here, we need to keep in mind that most of the books that have been named as religious scriptures are realisations of great men of this world. They attained this after much of self-contemplation and after delving deep inside.

It is natural for these scriptures to have some interpolations and addendums while recording those realisations and also because of the impact of time and intervals. Similarly, it is also possible that the person recording them might have failed himself to find enough words to describe the realisations. Further, it is also possible that disciples of those great men would have failed to understand the actual descriptions of their realisations in proper context or with real meaning. Those disciples would have deviated from the path that their spiritual heads would have trodden. In this regard, the fact that needs attention is that all those scriptures are being analysed and commented on by the people. This, in accordance with their understanding, their place, time and contemporary circumstances - be it the sayings of Vedic sages or sutras of Mahavira or teachings of Mahatma Buddha or thoughts of Jesus Christ or interpretations of Mohammed Sahab. The disciples of every great sage have always strived to use the name of their spiritual head and create an arrangement or grandiosity. They have intended to use to popularise their faith, cult, sect, temples, churches or madrasas. Who would not be aware of the fact that there are controversies today over the words of Jesus Christ? Not only that, we find a number of interpretations even for Islam that is believed to be initiated by Mohammed Sahab. There is lot of discord on the complexion of Islam that may be assumed to be consistent with the system and thinking that Hazarat Mohammed would have conceived with his own realisations. Probably, this may be the reason that in practice, the interpretation of Islam in Saudi Arabia does not match with that prevalent in Iran, Egypt and Turkey. The kind of Islam that we find in Malaysia is quite different from the same in many other Islamic countries. Why would have Shia and Sunni communities been in conflict if Islam were not communalised and people were not divided based on it?

The disciples of every great sage have always strived to use the name of their spiritual head and create an arrangement or grandiosity. They have intended to use to popularise their faith, cult, sect, temples and churches.

We find the same issue that exists with Islam, in such other faiths also that have been fabricated using the name of 'Dharma', in the guise of 'Dharma', for the protection of 'Dharma' or for the development of 'Dharma'. However, those frameworks have facilitated neither protection nor development of 'Dharma'. A real improvement in the behaviour of human beings and their eternal transformation only could be the best and most appropriate evidence of protection and development of 'Dharma'. The number of followers of a religious organisation or community or faith cannot be used as the criterion to decide whether 'Dharma' is progressing or not. In fact, the character of a person and development or decline of his moral values only can be taken as evidence of Dharma, nothing else.

If we ignore mankind, we may miss the most powerful support to express Dharma; we must, hence, keep mankind in the forefront whenever we discuss 'Dharma'. Unfortunately, human beings are often left far behind these days when discussing about Dharma. What comes to the front is ritualism, along with those systems, values and interpretations that are recorded in religious scriptures. Also what comes into focus, are those self-interests that are linked to temples, mosques, churches, monasteries, chaityas, gurudwaras and other places of worship. On the one hand, the number of temples, mosques, churches, chaityas, monasteries and other places of worship is ceaselessly increasing and innumerable idols of deities are being made. On the other, the people for whom all these things are being done are getting more narrow-minded, conservative, intolerant, unrighteous, restless and distraught. The way an average person interprets Dharma after reading religious scriptures and listening to mullahs, maulvis, priests, granthis and clerics, and the understanding that he possesses is indicative. It clearly indicates that he has turned more selfish, narrow-minded and ignorant compared to what he was earlier. We cannot claim that a person is really on the path of progress if he is turning parochial, conservative, communal and fanatical. We also cannot decide whether a person is really progressing based on his willingness to risk his life and indulge in violence for the sake of his religious belief. A person's development or his state of spirituality is not obvious even with the measure of his awareness, consciousness and diligence towards rituals, morals and codes of conduct scripted in books. Over-commitment towards rituals beyond certain limit makes a person inhuman and conservative. Too much of rituals does not help in real internal transformation. The darkness within a person does not get removed by rituals only. Rituals also do not help in making the nature

If we ignore mankind, we may miss the most powerful support to express Dharma; we must, hence, keep mankind in the forefront whenever we discuss 'Dharma'. Unfortunately, human beings are often left far behind these days.

of a person, benignant. The progress of a person can be determined only by ascertaining the levels of nectar and poison in the stream of flowing love and the source of humanity originating from his heart. People perform religious rituals, sadhana, worship, prayers and other experiments to discover this very stream of love. However, it has been observed very often that the person very soon deviates from his path. The main reason for this deviation is his ignorance of the real character of 'Dharma'. We may also say that when the person, instead of exploring inside, starts looking for Dharma in the outer world, his deviation starts increasing. Dharma is linked to the inner world. The person should have his conscience purified - that is what 'Rit Dharma' expects and that is what it aims for. Dharma connects with outer world also but only to a limited extent. The process of returning from outer world to the inner world, the effort made to understand the original character of self, all come under the purview of Dharma and that is its real form. What is happening in the human society for thousands of years is that man is trying to find and grab Dharma in the environment around him but he is not making attempts to look into his inner self.

> *The progress of a person can be determined only by ascertaining the levels of nectar and poison in the stream of flowing love and the source of humanity originating from his heart. People perform religious rituals, sadhana, worship and prayers.*

It is not at all possible for anyone to understand 'Dharma' deeply without uncovering the mysteries of self. And a person who is habituated to live with a personality imposed by the society would never be able to discover those mysteries. To understand one's self, a person would have to look into his inner self; he himself would have to realise the mysteries of his self. A person's self is ready to lay bare its mysteries to him only if he is ready to dive deep into inner world and to bring an end to his ego and eliminate it. If a person is unable to eliminate his ego, he would not be able to look into his inner self, and if a person is unable to look into his inner self, he would never be able to understand 'Dharma'. To uncover the mysteries of Dharma, it is necessary for a person to, first of all, get rid of all those preconceptions that have been imposed i.e. the conceptions that he has not perceived himself, like a scientist. How can a person explore himself if his mind is filled with preconceptions? How would he understand himself? The person who has blindly accepted other's perceptions as the best and started following it, cannot have his own perceptions. The person who is unable to realise his own perceptions would also not be able to find out the mysteries of 'Dharma'. To understand 'Dharma', it would have to be experienced by a person himself. Dharma is absolutely a personal matter, not a collective matter and that is the reason why 'Dharma' is also referred to as personal transformation. In human history, this transformation did not happen on a large scale but in a rare manner and has affected very few individuals; hence, a solution needs to be explored to make this transformation all-embracing.

The person who is unable to realise his own perceptions would also not be able to find out the mysteries of 'Dharma'. To understand 'Dharma', it would have to be experienced by a person himself.

If we go a little deep to ponder, it would be clear that the goal of 'Dharma' is the development of one's self and this development can take place only with own contemplation, cogitation, repeated meditation and practice. The point relates to recognition of the truth, the reality that the body is insignificant and consciousness is the prime thing. This consciousness appears to be related to body or external form. After some contemplation and practice, a situation comes when a person may have the realisation that consciousness cannot be fragmented. An individual's consciousness and Supreme consciousness do not have any difference but they appear to be different. It's like a person and his shadow - they do not have a separate existence though they appear to be separate. The core or the reality is the person only, not the shadow. Hence, till the time individual's consciousness treats itself to be separate from Supreme consciousness, it would function in a state of 'dualism' or 'separation'. This feeling of separation only is the biggest ignorance of a person. However, until that ignorance exists, the existence of separation would have to be accepted in our external life. Not one division but a series of divisions starts the moment the existence of separation is acknowledged. There is no way to avoid this series of divisions till the time a person remains in extroverted consciousness. This is the character of Param Chaitanya. This has been referred to by Indian philosophers as Chaitanya's 'lila' (sporting activity) or 'enjoyment'.

'Dharma' is an effective endeavour to take us away from ignorance. This is a successful remedy for mental and intellectual dizziness. However, this remedy certainly needs to be applied in different ways on different patients. Every individual has a unique mental and intellectual framework; hence the condition of ailment of ignorance also would be unique for an individual. That is the reason that the remedy for ignorance is impossible with the help of collective Dharma or treatment or medicine. Unfortunately, collective treatment is prevalent even today in the name of Dharma. This collective treatment makes a person communal and that is the reason why the psychology of the crowd becomes dominant on the individual. This psychology of the crowd has brought down 'Dharma' from its high level of consciousness, instead of making it clean, clear and transparent.

The external ambience and symbols like temples, mosques and churches created in the name of 'Dharma' can be helpful to a limited extent only when they are used for understanding al l-pervading consciousness.

That day is sure to come when a person would realise that 'Dharma' is actually linked to internal purification. Internal purification does not require mobocracy. Contemplation and cogitation on internal purification can be done only after getting into the silence of solitude. This solitude is also absolutely personal and is linked to mind and intellect. More than the solitude of environment, what is needed is mental solitude and mental silence. It is not at all possible for a person to enter the laboratory of 'Dharma' in the absence of mental solitude and silence.

The external ambience and symbols like temples, mosques and churches created in the name of 'Dharma' can be helpful to a limited extent only when they are used for understanding all-pervading consciousness. External symbols have very limited significance in respect of a person's internal development. Generally, the external symbols become instruments for inciting division and communalism in society. They also create obstacles in the contemplation of the Supreme Oneness, as these symbols get linked to political, economic and social self-interests. The moment a symbol gets linked to self-interest and self-importance, it ceases to be a carrier of the consciousness of the Supreme One. Rather, it becomes a divider for the consciousness. Here in, starts the suffering inflicted on mankind in the name of 'Dharma'.

The consciousness of Dharma cannot be blamed for the controversy that exists in respect of 'Dharma'. If a person really looks into his inner self under consciousness of Dharma, the realisation that he would achieve after delving deep inside would never be inconsistent. It would not be inconsistent because only a person who has completely renounced the existence of self would be able to delve deep inside self and inside consciousness. If there remains a bit of the existence of separation, if there is a trace of affliction of ego, there would be an equal amount of ego, self-interest and also narrow-mindedness in whatever is achieved with it. The truth in ego-centred realisation gets afflicted with distraction. If a person desires to really enter the consciousness of Dharma, he may have to get rid of everything and turn himself into a complete naught. With consciousness of the existence of the self still present, whatever is concluded would be just a belief or thought and that would not convey a message of Supreme Oneness.

The consciousness of Dharma cannot be blamed for the controversy that exists in respect of 'Dharma'.

'Dharma' is controversial only because it has been influenced by ego. When experience, realisation, thinking and rituals are imposed on a person in the name of devotion, faith and belief, and organisations and institutions are established to safeguard them, controversies will occur. Those who have understood the real truth would never have difference of opinion, as truth cannot have two different versions. Certainly, there may be multiple ways to view the truth and multiple paths to reach it. However, existence of dissimilarities in the paths to attain truth does not mean that truth would have multiple versions. Whatever be the truth, when a seeker attains it with perseverance, contemplation and karma, his condition is similar to the wave that merges with ocean aiming to discover the ocean. There exists neither the viewer nor the view nor the vision, once truth is attained. Still, when the person, lying deep in this consciousness or transformed from that state, re-enters this common world, back from his world of imagination. This also means, the person returns to the consciousness of separation (consciousness of viewer, view and vision), and is unable, with whatever memory he is left with, to define that truth with appropriate words. If an attempt is made to assign words to the realisation, they get impacted by the place, period and perspective. This again is one of the reasons for the variances in opinion, which exist in the name of 'Dharma'.

The controversy raised in the name of 'Dharma' actually reinforces immorality and takes a person and society far away from the consciousness of 'Dharma'.

The controversies on 'Dharma' may also attract a comment that when we use consciousness of Dharma under the influence of ego, our arrogance overshadows the predominantly true consciousness of Dharma. This is indisputable that where there is predominance of arrogance, controversies would definitely get raised. There can be no way to evade controversies while being in the consciousness of arrogance. Arrogance is the reason for self-interest to get in; it also allows development of the fear that our self-interests may get hurt. This fear helps and even inspires us to organise, construct ramparts and walls and establish defence structures. This very psyche works behind the division that exists, the walls that are erected and the sects that are formed in the name of 'Dharma'.

The controversy raised in the name of 'Dharma' actually reinforces immorality and takes a person and society far away from the consciousness of 'Dharma'. The person instigating division and debates in the name of 'Dharma' and the person recognising separation in the guise of 'Dharma' can never be righteous. Here also, there is a need to be careful about extremism. There is a need to be careful because there is possibility of misuse of real tolerance and magnanimity of 'Dharma'. And this, to facilitate the emergence of such powers that intend to demolish righteousness and consciousness of Dharma. This vigilance would certainly be required in the consciousness of dualism in outer world, as consciousness of the world cannot be maintained by diving into complete righteous consciousness.

Thus, even though it is known that truth and realisation are unique, we may have to recognise separation in the domain of Dharma, as the 'complete human' is yet to be born. A lot has to be done and remarkable progress has to be realised to help humans achieve their fullness. The destination is still far away. In these circumstances, we may have to accept the principle of 'live and let live' and move ahead in our lives.

□

3

Dharma and Paramatma

No other subject or matter has generated the kind of debates, contemplation, cogitation and bloodshed that have taken place on account of Dharma and Paramatma i.e. Supreme Being. What is the relation of Dharma with Paramatma? Is Paramatma accessible only to a righteous person? Who is a righteous person? Would absence of Dharma block all the paths leading to Paramatma? Is it necessary to deliberate on Dharma for spiritual progress to be possible? Is spirituality the Dharma and is Dharma the spirituality? Does Paramatma have any Dharma just like a human being? What about the status of existence of a person who does not want to reach Paramatma by following Dharma or who wants to understand neither Dharma not Paramatma? Would a human being lose his right to live on this earth if he refuses to accept the existence of Paramatma? Who would define and interpret what is Dharma and what is Paramatma? And if anybody does provide interpretation for it, what would be the criteria to validate if that interpretation only is true and correct? Is there any proof to show that Dharma is linked to Paramatma? Is there any proof to confirm there is a special or separate existence of Paramatma and Dharma has been invented to reach there? There is no surety how many such questions are there that are connected to this subject. Every human being has the liberty to interpret these questions according to his own understanding. However, this is definite that wandering about with endless queries would help in understanding neither Dharma and Paramatma nor the relationship between Dharma and Paramatma, if any. A brain concerned only in raising questions may ultimately create a condition of insanity but cannot provide any solution. It is normal to raise questions for understanding a subject, but finding a solution becomes impossible if we get entangled in questions only. Reasoning beyond a limit becomes sophism and sophism erodes rationality, it does not support the later. Beyond questions and reasoning is the state of cogitation, contemplation, practice, behaviour and examination. It's not possible to attain the knowledge of Dharma and even Paramatma without diving into the ocean of behaviour. Neither is Dharma an intellectual amusement nor does Paramatma become accessible with too much of reasoning or too many questions.

What is Dharma? This has been interpreted so many times and in so many ways that it does not look possible to define it in a new way, at least today. That something new may be added to that interpretation; the same may be said about interpretation of 'Paramatma' also. Even after all this, it cannot be said today that the ultimate truth, ultimate interpretation has been uncovered. Indian philosophy recognises that the structure of Dharma is infinite and Paramatma is also non-dual and infinite. Infinite can never be interpreted completely and conclusively. Infinite can never be understood in a constitutive or affirmative state.

> *What is Dharma? This has been interpreted so many times and in so many ways that it does not look possible to define it in a new way,at least today. That something new may be added to that interpretation.*

Completeness of infinite cannot be understood even after having the knowledge of whatever is available or whatever has been achieved, as the real form of infinite would remain unknowable due to its boundlessness even after knowing 'everything'. Neither Dharma nor Paramatma can be understood without understanding the mystery of this 'Unknowable'. Dharma and Paramatma are not unknown even in their completeness, but they are surely unknowable. Unknown refers to that about which nothing is known and unknowable means that the subject is known, it has been felt and realised also, but still a lot remains to be known and a lot would remain to be known always. Indian sages refer this state of truth as 'नेति-नेति' i.e. 'not this, not this'.

As Dharma and Paramatma have infinite forms, their different forms would attract different responses from a human mind and these responses would only build its commitment. Commitment means devotion to a specific interpretation and idea. If this devotion is imperfect, the commitment also would be imperfect and if devotion is absolute, the commitment also would be absolute. When a person assumes himself to be highly knowledgeable about 'Dharma' and 'Paramatma' and attempts to impose his thoughts, beliefs, interpretations and opinions upon society, this becomes a reason for a community to emerge. This situation even makes a common person and his followers' intransigent. The same mentality has been the reason for emergence of pig-headedness and superstition. This hyper-commitment only makes a society conservative and a hypnotised with rigidity and extremism, closing all doors for new ideas, reasoning and solutions. Mankind has not been able to find a remedy and solution yet to this psychological problem. Though, it cannot be said that there is no solution to this problem; a solution does exist. This cannot be found without ridding mankind of independent and preconceived thinking. When a person enters this domain, treating others' thoughts, experiences and perceptions as his own, he stays unconscious mentally and intellectually, though remaining conscious physically. This very unconsciousness is his intellectual trance, and a person under an intellectual trance would eventually perceive neither truth nor Dharma nor Paramatma.

Dharma can never take a collective form in its subtlety. Dharma can be embraced only in its individualised form; the moment Dharma attains collective form, it loses its original character and is left as 'karmakand'.

Dharma can never take a collective form in its subtlety. Dharma can be embraced only in its individualised form; the moment Dharma attains collective form, it loses its original character and is left as 'karmakand'. After getting into collectiveness, Dharma is either 'karmakand' or customs and manners that are also called as 'rituals' in English. All these - karmakand, ceremonies, customs and manner and 'rituals' are linked to specific conventions as well as some specific beliefs. In this state, Dharma loses its original beauty and meaning. This kind of 'adapted Dharma' breaks up the society into multiple parts, divides humanity, makes it communal. The approach makes a person parochial and conservative, instead of being helpful in awakening of spiritual consciousness.

The deep desire and thirst to find out the Whole and understand the truth is also a form of Dharma. This very desire born out of Dharma takes a person close to Paramatma. This very thirst eventually prompts every human being towards divinity. The thirst, the desire to know Paramatma i.e. the Supreme Soul i.e. one that is Supreme, infinite and eternal is the main motive for development of the inner self of a person. The ignorance and darkness of the inner self can be eliminated only when the person has real desire and intense thirst to know the supreme truth. The intensity of this thirst only is the secret behind his success. This very intensity would be his torch-bearer and the path also would be paved with the same intensity, though the intensity here is absolutely personal. There is no way to ensure that two persons feel thirst with the same intensity. Even under the same circumstances, two experiences can never be identical in entirety. This distinctness arises due to differences in the framework of minds. Here, it is worth noting that every person has a unique level of intensity of thirst and also unique limit for its quenching. Some people are satisfied with a small amount, whereas others remain unsatisfied with it. Every person has his own level of spiritual, mental and intellectual energy. The uniqueness of these spiritual, mental and intellectual levels only create the personality of an individual. This only forms his mental faculty, character and behaviour, also depending on his own spiritual, mental and intellectual forces. When two persons do not have same character, mental faculty and mental & intellectual force, their Dharma also should be distinct. The decision for the path to be chosen by a particular person for 'Dharma' i.e. spiritual development has to be carved by him only and then only he would find his correct path. This is the reason that Indian philosophy recognises Dharma as personal

There is no way to ensure that two persons feel thirst with the same intensity. Even under the same circumstances, two experiences can never be identical in entirety. This distinctness arises due to differences in the framework of minds.

karma and personal consciousness. What is 'my Dharma' cannot be 'your Dharma'; however, the West did not allow the understanding of Dharma to be developed in this way. The West considers that if 'Dharma' does exist, it is not dependent on an individual, rather it depends on class and community. In the West, Dharma is linked to external consciousness. There, the path of Dharma is defined only by some specific great personality and general people are motivated and hypnotised to follow the same path. This very disposition of Western thinking has proved be the most fertile ground for communalism. However, communalism may get developed anywhere. If groups get created with persons who understand 'Dharma' only as 'personal consciousness' or 'personal disposition', that situation may also give rise to communalism. However, despite being true, this is not a reality, as the persons who create their own groups do not have full faith in their thinking. A group is formed only when individuals are victims of fear and ignorance. Such persons do talk of totality, morality and Dharma but their inner selves are not illuminated fully. Half-baked belief cannot be called truth or total faith. Only a person who does not suffer from a credibility gap would be a complete devotee. If every individual owns his special 'private Dharma', he would be confidently treading his path to find out supreme truth with the help of his 'private Dharma'. In that situation, he would not even think of interfering with the 'private Dharma' of others. Thoughts of conflict and interference would develop only when they get some fertile land for it. If a deep desire has developed fully in the mind of a person to awaken from the state of trance and if he has become too restless with the thirst to find out supreme truth, he would concentrate only on his aim to quench his thirst. He is unable to see or hear anything other than his aim of quenching spiritual thirst - this only is the real state of mind under the deepest and supreme thirst. 'Dharma' born out of this state of mind and restless consciousness would be virtuous only, and that only would be truth-oriented Dharma, as

However, communalism may get developed anywhere. If groups get created with persons who understand 'Dharma' only as 'personal consciousness' or 'personal disposition'.

also karma-oriented Dharma. That only would be called truth-soaked duty, a duty that is not performed with the notion of duty, rather that is performed with natural self-motivation. Real spiritual duty is not performed, rather it is something that arises from deep within and is a natural action that gets done automatically every moment. For example, the Sun does not perform a duty of spreading light, it just spreads light because that is its character. Just like spreading light is an identification of the existence of sun, a real 'divine human being' also must have some identification. This very 'divine human' is the complete human and this complete human is the manifestation of the Supreme Soul. This Supreme Soul, this complete human can be neither communal nor intransigent nor parochial nor conservative. This very complete human is the consummation of the development of mankind. This is the last stage of human development. We all are marching ahead to become complete human beings with the help of our character and our individual 'private Dharma'. This is happening whether anybody accepts this or not.

Real spiritual duty is not performed,rather it is something that arises from deepwithin and is a natural action that gets done automaticalIy every moment. For example,the Sun does not perform a duty ofspreading light,it just spreads light.

Every human being gets some inkling of his incompleteness from somewhere and then gets restless to eliminate it. That being, works in that direction, marches ahead and gives sometimes entire and sometimes part of his life force to eliminate his incompleteness. The extent of the life force applied for eliminating insufficiency and incompleteness determines the extent of one's achievement. Any resolve backed with full life force can never remain unfulfilled, but rarely anybody is ready to give his full force. To thrust one's full force means effacing himself at all levels and taking the shape of that resolve himself. That person does not give importance to his own ego-centric existence, rather he awakes, sleeps and moves around as resolve personified and his all works get created, unveiled and derived from his resolve only.

This incompleteness of a person exists at any or at all levels. A normal person is incomplete at all levels - body, life, intellect, spirit.

This incompleteness is not his real character, but as he is in a state of fully or partly incoherent consciousness instead of live consciousness, he treats himself incomplete despite being complete. He then keeps trying to eliminate his incompleteness. The best thinking of Indian philosophy is that only complete existence is all-pervasive; if you take out full from full, you would be left with full; if you add full to full, you would be still left with full. The complete would always be undivided. There is no difference between a wave and an ocean; ocean is the wave and wave is the ocean. Incompleteness is only apparent. In reality, incompleteness can never exist. Incompleteness becomes apparent only because the wave has started to treat itself separate from the ocean. This very ignorance of the wave is the cause for its grief, its turmoil, its pain, its struggle and its excitement. The day that wave understands its real character, all separation, entire incompleteness, all shortages would vanish; but this knowledge, this realisation, though appearing simple, does not come easily. In order to attain this realisation only, a person makes all kinds of attempts unconsciously or naturally or eventually under compulsion. Until the ignorance of a person is eliminated, he would remain restless and keep agonising. All endeavours, all attempts to remove incompleteness, to eliminate ignorance and to attain completeness are considered to be 'Dharma'.

The best thinking of Indian philosophy is that only complete existence is all-pervasive; if you take out full from full, you would be left with full; if you add full to full, you would be still left with full. The complete would always be undivided.

The mystery of Dharma thus becomes all the more complicated as a person is not aware of different levels of his own consciousness. However, attempts are continued to be made, sometime naturally and sometime with specific effort, for elimination of incompleteness that exists at each level of consciousness. This complication further goes up when the karma required for one level of consciousness is repeated for other levels also, unconsciously, ignorantly or naturally. This also happens because our exploration of self-i.e. exploration of inner self is very limited and incomplete. Hence, it is the endeavour of Dharma to encourage an individual to first of all be aware of himself, explore his inner self and understand that level of his consciousness for which or from where, he wishes to perform karma. His consciousness would slowly get rid of darkness and he would come out of his trance only after exploring the inner self faithfully. Once a person comes out of his trance, he does not perform karma for himself or his self-interest or even for the benefit of others. Karma is definitely performed by such a person but still it cannot be said that he is performing it. Such a person only slowly gets conscious, awakens, separates from the existence of body i.e. existence of dualism and merges with the Whole. This state attained after merging with the Whole is something similar to the state of the Supreme Soul, the Supreme Consciousness. Whatever is there, or not there - that can be expressed neither by words nor by experience nor by perception. This is the Paramatma, this is the Supreme Power and this is the Divinity. This is the Whole, this is Bramha and this only is the Param Ananda i.e. bliss.

Karma is definitely performed by such a person but still it cannot be said that he is performing it. Such a person only slowly gets conscious, awakens,separates from the existence of body i.e. existence of dualism.

For mankind, the search for Paramatma is a natural search. This very search is also called the search for God. Search for Paramatma or search for God or search for Param Chaitanya - there is no difference among them. A wave would be at peace only when it merges with the ocean again. Every wave rises only to be merged with the ocean, which is its aim, its nature and its Dharma. All the anxiety of a part or a fragment is for the goal of identifying its completeness. The part is not a part and the fragment is not a fragment in real sense, as completeness cannot be fragmented. If ignorance does exist, that would certainly get eliminated. Why is there ignorance? Where did the conviction of fragmentation come from? Why did complete get occupied by incomplete? How can one who is himself incomplete know answers to all these questions? The incomplete would certainly meet the complete someday. However, none of the parts, fragments and incompletes would ever know what is complete, as the complete is infinitely infinite. The complete is so colossal that it has no end, no border, and no means to know if there is any end or border. The complete is infinite and colossal that cannot be understood by the fragment, the part and the incomplete. That is what is referred to as Param Bramha by Indian philosophy, that is Paramatma and that is that colossal great void which encompasses everything. The way to understand this character of consciousness can be found only through 'Dharma'.

It is a misconception of mankind that understanding Paramatma, the Supreme Being does not depend on him. Every inanimate and living object would have to develop itself and in all cases, it would eventually find out Paramatma. To understand Paramatma, to awaken from the state of unconsciousness is the destiny of every person. Every inanimate and living object, every part and fragment, whatever is there and whatever is not there. Whatever has happened and whatever may happen, all of them would have to eventually enter the consciousness of Bramha. Somewhat like this only, can be described in words.

To understand Paramatma,to awaken from the state of unconsciousness is the destiny of every person. Every inanimate and living object,every part and fragment,whatever is there and whatever is not there.

Those who say that they are atheists and do not believe in Paramatma, they are actually under a misconception only and still in a state of semi-delirium. Ultimately, it is not in the hands of a believer or an atheist to awaken and understand Paramatma or not to understand Paramatma or merge into the existence of Bramha, the divine consciousness. An atheist may say anything, but ultimately he would reach his origin and attain his completeness. He only claims that an idol is not Bramha and believes that there is no Paramatma that resides beyond our universe or that comes to life out of an idol. An atheist only thinks that there is no creator of this visible world, and that happiness and grief are not under divine control, rather they are creations of humans only. He also thinks that he would ultimately be able to uncover the mystery of life and death in his laboratory. According to him, fortune-maker for the mankind is nothing other than the worldly prosperity. The atheist provides many more arguments like these. These however don't prove that there is no existence of the supreme truth, nor can they prove that there is no all-pervading divine force in this world. Nor can they prove that the force that exists is uncontrolled, indisciplined and anarchic. The entire energy of an atheist remains busy in proving that only a human being is a living entity and this natural world is inanimate and has many mysteries. This natural world is working under discipline and that man is unravelling those mysteries one-by-one with the help of his intelligence and winning over the nature and its mysteries. Superficially, this argument of an atheist is valid, but if we look a bit deeper, the atheist would look to be entangled in his own web of arguments. The latest discoveries of science have already proved that an electric energy is streaming continuously not only in our solar system but in the entire universe. This electric energy is the fundamental element of this entire universe. All inanimate and living objects, existing on this earth or anywhere else, are forms of this energy only. Even a stone that is the most inanimate object, is made of the atoms that, if split further, provide electrical energy in the end. A stone that is considered inanimate is also a condensed form of energy. What is the source of that electrical energy which is spread across the entire universe? Science does not have any answer to this. What is called electrical energy by science is referred to as consciousness or eternal force. The entire universe is flooded with an infinitely infinite ocean of electrical energy. Not only nebulas, stars, constellations, solar system, earth and inanimate and animate objects but even the things expressed or unexpressed are the same, perpetually flowing unsegmented electrical energy. This infinite electrical energy prevalent in the all-pervading whole is referred to as Supreme Bramha in philosophical language - whatever name an atheist gives to the same is up to him. The name does not make any difference. The total of everything in this all-pervading whole is Paramatma only. The separation that is felt by the atheist because of his

The entire universe is flooded with an infinitely infinite ocean ofelectrical energy. Not only nebulas, stars,constel lations, solar system,earth and inanimate and animate objects but even the things expressed.

own ego and impacted or operated by place, time and circumstances, is not a reality, though it appears to be real. The fact is that a wave is a part of ocean only and the fundamental element, permanent and eternal element is the ocean only and not the wave. Fundamentally, there is no difference between a wave and the ocean.

An atheist and a believer would not have any dispute or objection with regard to this scientific character of consciousness. An atheist has objection to individualist God and Paramatma. Priests and clerics linked the conception of the 'Supreme Consciousness' to the idea of an individualist God and created a problem for the mankind. These priests and ritualists have presented the existence of God as autocratic and irrational sovereign loving sycophancy. This individualist God of priests and ritualists may be pleased with prayers, worships and offerings. This kind of individualist and sycophancy-loving God offers heaven only to those who make offerings and worship persistently. Those who are not good at sycophancy are sent to hell. This individualist God, who has the power to decide on heaven and hell, happiness and grief, life and death, award and punishment, has created many difficulties for humanity. As this individualist God got linked to economic and political self-interests of a certain class of people. This individualist God has made humans narrow-minded, conservative, selfish and communalist.

> *An atheist and a believer would not have any dispute or objection with regard to this scientific character of consciousness. An atheist has objection to individualist God and Paramatma. Priests and clerics linked.*

The fact is that the main reasons behind priestification and politicisation of 'Dharma' have been the imaginary ideas in respect of God. These imaginary ideas propagated in the form of deism have been successful in attracting an immature mind. Also, the ritualism suggested for associating with this deism or **prophetism or priestism has also been named 'Dharma'. This priest or angel or prophet-oriented thinking has divided mankind into several beliefs, opinions, heresies and faiths and each segment, assigned the name of a separate Dharma. Every prophet, every angel and every deist**

started to refer to their beliefs, their thinking and their rituals as 'Dharma' and this only polluted the word 'Dharma'.

In reality, Dharma has nothing to do with this priestism or prophetism or anthropomorphism. Dharma is above all of them. This truth was understood by the saints and sages of India; their invaluable opinions and thoughts are available even today in the form of Upanishads. Unfortunately, proper discussions on them and their correct interpretations are not being done. To establish Dharma in its pure and enlightened form, it is necessary to protect it from superstitions, anthropomorphism, priestism, popeism and prophetism. The aim of Dharma is to purify one's inner self. Dharma is the name of the art to orient the consciousness towards divinity. It facilitates knowledge of omnisciency, all-pervasiveness and oneness of the Supreme Being i.e. Paramatma. It also helps the consciousness of a person to awaken from trance and enter into a state of perpetual awareness and complete alertness. The more a person awakens his consciousness, the more he reaches closer to Chaitanya i.e. the Consciousness or the Supreme Being. Awakening of consciousness means moving from darkness towards light. Getting oneself free from the bondage of egotism is the first stage of awakening of his consciousness. Dharma only provides a person the ways to freedom from his ego and helps him progress towards divinity.

In reality,Dharma has nothing to do with this priestism or prophetism or anthropomorphism. Dharma is above al l of them. This truth was understood by the saints and sages of India; their invaluable opinions and thoughts are available.

Dharma is a transformation, an inner enlightenment, a means for inner journey and a process to understand oneself. If a person attempts to understand the world without knowing himself, he would stray away from his path and would be restless and agitated. Mankind has been restless in every generation and is restless even today. The main reason for it is that they do not want to introspect and almost refuse to take up the inner journey and traverse their inner selves. One who cannot go through the inner journey cannot be righteous. Dharma is the art of transformation of inner self, is a method of inflaming the inner light to help eliminate all depravity, win over the darkness and enter the state of bliss. Such a state of bliss cannot be experienced with asceticism. That divine bliss cannot be realised by inflicting suffering to oneself, by burning or melting, beating or by baking oneself. To pursue the path of divinity, it is essential for the person to recognise himself, and a person who tortures himself, bakes himself, and cannot recognise his own real character.

Dharma is not a noun rather it is a verb, and hence whenever we discuss it or think of it, we should reflect over it only in the form of action. Dharma means living a righteous life. Its purpose is to adopt righteousness in all aspects of life. Righteousness is an inner enlightenment and related to inner awakening. Perpetual awareness towards inner self and alertness towards Chaitanya is the real righteousness. This very conscious awakening is the real energy and force of a person. Dharma i.e. righteousness takes us towards conscious awakening, and frees us from superstitions. Conscious awakening means our alertness towards perpetually flowing consciousness, and our complete awareness towards all-pervading existence of the Supreme Being. It also includes our consciousness that one existence and only one Supreme Being is present everywhere. Whatever inanimate or animate objects are there, they are nowhere and no way separate from it and all are inseparable parts of one only. It is our ignorance only to refer something or accept it as separate. Dharma destroys this very ignorance and in this sense, it is 'the Destroyer' Shiva. It is the Lord of time and it is also death. This form of death is meant to assign a new dimension to the existence of Creation. Death only is the first step of creation. If there were no deaths, no new creation would be possible. Creation only is the Dharma of death. He, who becomes conscious of this righteousness, wins over his ignorance, his restlessness and finds the door that leads to the eternal bliss. If there is any God or Paramatma, it is there in that 'Bliss' only. I do not know what

Dharma is not a noun rather it is a verb, and hence whenever we discuss it or think of it, we should reflect over it only in the form of action. Dharma means living a righteous life. Its purpose is to adopt righteousness in all aspects of life.

kind of happiness that bliss provides. I am also not aware if anybody else knows that; but this can be certainly said that entire grief ceases under that bliss and there is no sadness, no death and no fragmented life there.

If mankind is to be changed, transformed, their misery is to end, led to peace, moral instincts are to be developed and if he have to experience bliss, they will have to embrace righteousness within themselves. If 'Dharma' embraces any ideology, some rituals, refers to any such procedure that might help in acquiring different kinds of material happiness for our external life. As also, protecting us from detrimental consequences of even our crimes, that it is not 'Dharma' in real sense. Rather it is superstition, hypocrisy and such an order that does not help in inner enlightenment. Any amount of prayers and worship with an inner-self filled with darkness would not help a person attain righteousness. Another bitter truth is also there that any visualisation of Bhagavan or Ishvara or Paramatma separate from self is just a fantasy or superstition that has been prevalent for thousands of years. If we decide even once to accept any Bhagavan or Ishvara or Paramatma separate from self, we only attempt to limit Param Chaitanya, the Supreme Divinity, the Supreme Being. One that is complete, unlimited and infinitely infinite, how can that be limited? Bhagavan is neither a person nor any such special extra-terrestrial existence that is separate from the whole, this creation, and the inanimate and livings objects. We are not sure how many bhagavans, ishvaras and paramatmas have been created during the last thousands of years just in the guise of 'Dharma'. They have been the reasons for thousands of battles, immeasurable bloodshed and endless injustice and exploitation. If we have to get rid of battles, bloodshed, injustice and exploitation, we would have to get rid of 'Bhagavan', 'Ishvara' or 'Paramatma' present in any form separate from self.

> *If there is any God or Paramatma, it is there in that 'Bliss' only. I do not know what kind of happiness that bliss provides. I am also not aware if anybody else knows that; but this can be certainly said that entire grief ceases under that bliss.*

The need of the hour is not that a new bhagavan or ishvara or paramatma is given shape; there is also no need to pick one of those bhagavans, ishvaras and paramatmas and get them recognised by the entire mankind. The only thing that is needed at this moment is that the mankind becomes introspective, reflects into their inner selves and recognises the truth that there is only one Chaitanya that is all pervading. This Chaitanya is perpetual, infinite and universal. It is complete and total - 'Whatever I am is the world'! What is needed is that there should be an inner enlightenment such that we might be able to seethe the all-pervading Supreme Being, divinity, supreme soul. In fact, not only see but get immersed in it, adapt to it and get transformed completely. Mankind does not need any God separate from himself; he only needs inner enlightenment of perpetual, whole and complete Supreme Being. Real Dharma points to this very process and arrangement. After getting the indication and understanding it, every person would have to find his own path, light his lamp and be his torchbearer and guru himself, to reach that complete divinity, the Supreme Being.

Dharma does provide some idea ofthe process to jumpinto the unknown,but leaves it to the person making that jumpi.e. the inquisitive person to whichever art he wants to use for that jump. Self-realisation or enlightenment cannot.

One more point that needs to be understood properly is that the connection of Dharma with prayers, worship, chants, meditations, austerity, etc. is very basic. It is so basic that a person may attain righteousness and reach Supreme Being even without worship, prayers and chants. These cannot be referred to as Dharma - all these activities are just rituals that may give rise to curiosity in our minds to know and experience it. Prayers and worship may help us reach that door after which starts the domain of Dharma. However, we may need to be ready for a long jump after reaching that door. We would make this jump deep within ourselves. A peculiar thing here is that we would feel uncertainty all around, as the place where we are making the jump is not known to us, rather we may say that we have to jump into the unknown. Dharma does provide some idea of the process to jump into the unknown, but leaves it to the person making that jump i.e. the inquisitive person to whichever art he wants to use for that jump. Self-realisation or enlightenment cannot be attained without making that jump, and Paramatma i.e. the Supreme Being is beyond reach without that enlightenment. One more point that needs to be understood is that the purpose of that jump is not only to attain self-realisation or reach Paramatma. Rather, in this series of objectives, the first objective would be elimination of self, complete elimination of ego, end of dualism and death of 'I'. Until the existence of 'I' is demolished and not a trace of existence of dualism remains, Paramatma would not even appear. Here, the reference to appearance of Paramatma is not a very correct expression of this ideological situation. Paramatma is omnipresent, neither has he gone anywhere, nor is he hiding nor is he lost; but until dualism oriented consciousness is predominant, he cannot be understood. When the existence of 'I' is gone and the feeling of dualism is not there and only the existence of Paramatma remains, only then Paramatma becomes accessible. In reality, there is nothing like sighting the Paramatma, his attainment, appearance or reincarnation. They are not reality because he is all pervading and eternal. But, this realisation of truth, this consciousness can happen only when a person gets fully awakened, conscious and transformed on the levels of his mind and inner self. A wave cannot understand the ocean; the wave just merges with it and becomes the ocean itself. The moment the realisation of a separate existence of wave is lost, the reality of the ocean and its existence become apparent. Dharma is that knowledge that provides the way to go past the notion of ego i.e. the sense of dualism. Only beyond that sense of dualism exists all the pervading infinitely infinite Chaitanya, the Supreme Being, the Supreme Soul. That very existence is the truth, that only is the knowledge, which only is eternal, is nectar and that only is new Dharma.

The moment the realisation of a separate existence of wave is lost, the reality of the ocean and its existence become apparent. Dharma is that knowledge that provides the way to go past the notion of ego i.e. the sense of dualism.

4

Existence and Sanatana Dharma

If there is any existence, it must be having some character. Existence can be identified only by its character. There are two forms of an existence. In one of the forms, its attributes are apparent and these attributes only make others aware of its existence. The existence is perceived in one another way also and that is through its works and its accomplishments. Every existence would certainly have some character and some accomplishments. Accomplishments also would be such that they specifically identify that existence. This character and these accomplishments only are the Dharma of that existence.

It is an indisputable fact that if there is an existence, there exists its Dharma. This form of Dharma is manifested not by its name but by action. If there is an eternal existence, its activities also would be eternal. If the existence is momentary, is volatile, its activities also would be momentary and volatile only.

The actuality of existence may be divided into two forms. One of the forms of existence is that which is infinite, unabridged and beyond interpretation. This form of existence is impossible to be understood completely. Only a glimpse of this eternal existence may be experienced-that also only with the consciousness of the inner self; anything beyond this is not possible. This existence that is infinite, unabridged or whole and all pervading, appears to be impossible to be interpreted. How big is this existence? How small is it? Is it liquid or solid? Is it inanimate or living? Where does it start from and where does it end? What are its dimensions? How big is its area of dominance? 'That exists' - only this can be realised as a glimpse in the consciousness of the inner self and that also only sometimes; nothing more in respect with it can be understood. 'That exists' - this knowledge itself is enough to provide a perception of the 'existence'. It is remarkable to note that the one who needs to realise or perceive this eternal existence or who is already in the process of realising this eternal existence, is himself an extremely short-lived, momentary and tiny form of this existence. How can one who is himself momentary and extremely minute, understand the eternal and colossal existence? The same thing can be also expressed in this way - one that is infinite cannot be understood by finite. The very mention of infinite indicates that it is an existence that has no border, no boundary and no edge. Such an existence would always remain unknown. Indian philosophers treat this unknown as the Supreme Bramha. Whatever is in contact with our senses or our feeling or has already come in contact with them or might come in contact with them anytime in future, is the only. The one 'That exists', that means that existence also is only a small part of the infinite existence. This is the maximum that the words may express to introduce or interpret Bramha.

Indian philosophers treat this unknown as the Supreme Bramha. Whatever is in contact with our senses or our feeling or has already come in contact with them or might come in contact with them anytime in future.

On the other side, the second form of existence is that character of the consciousness of Supreme Bramha that, though undivided, appears to be divided or diverse. Consciousness expresses itself in two ways - it is introvert and at the same time extrovert also. When consciousness is extrovert, it gets impacted and divided by place, time and shape. This extrovert consciousness only is the creator of time. It is the ego of this consciousness that links it to shape and place in addition to time. This extrovert consciousness born out of ego has the nature to expand itself. Ego can never remain without expansion. In a sense, expansion is the Dharma of ego. Today, whatever mankind refers to as the expansion of Mother Nature is actually the egoism of the 'Param Chaitanya', this is its Dharma and shape also. This extrovert world has innumerable forms - they are known in inanimate forms as well as in living forms. These forms, though being undivided and unabridged, appears to be divided and fragmented and have separate existence. They certainly possess a fundamental character, which makes it possible to perceive the existence of that specific form. As example, the existence of water is an expansion of 'Param Bramha'. Sovereignty of the existence of water is known by its liquidity and its capacity to wet, hence it can be said that liquidity and its capacity to wet only is the fundamental Dharma of water. This second aspect of existence, though not true, appears to be true to mankind as it is the character of existence of inanimate and animate born out of division of every Chaitanya. And though not separate, appear to be separate and, though not true, appear to be true. We call this in short as fundamental nature. This nature also in reality is Bramha only but appears to be separate from Bramha in extrovert consciousness. Why this existence of nature, though not separate, appears to be separate? Nobody has been able to answer this and perhaps this cannot be answered also. Param Chaitanya divides itself or appears divided, for its own interest, for its own enjoyment - only this can be understood. This character of Bramha is eternal. This eternal character only is the source of Dharma and, in this context, the existence of Dharma also is perpetual, eternal and ubiquitous.

This second aspect of existence,though not true,appears to be true to mankind as it is the character of existence of inanimate and animate born out of division of every Chaitanya.

This form of existence of Dharma is constant as, if this Dharma is gone, existence also would be lost. If a thing is not wet or is not liquid, we cannot claim that it is 'water'. It's the Dharma of water to wet; hence till the time a liquid substance wets, it would be called water. It is not possible even to imagine water without the Dharma of wetness. In this sense, Dharma here is constant and eternal, but there is also another form that is influenced and operated by mind. 'Dharma' influenced and operated by mind would be changeable just like the mind. The mind is a perpetually changeable existence by its character. This is the reason that Indian philosophers assume nature to be flickering as the existence of nature depends on mind. Whatever comes under the existence of nature and its boundaries is time-barred, hence its birth and death keeps occurring perpetually. This cyclic motion is the fundamental character of nature and in that sense, continuous change in this cyclic motion is the course as well as Dharma of nature.

Perception of the existence of Dharma in extrovert life is also popular in a different form. This form of Dharma is so individual centric and self-interest centric that Dharma loses its perpetuity here and starts getting directed and impacted by place, time and circumstances. Dharma, in this form, resides within the periphery of the wheel of time. Whatever comes within the periphery of the wheel of time would not be perpetual rather it would be continuously changeable only. On the contrary, the navel of this wheel of time and the extremely minute central point of that wheel is always static. It does not have any motion. This very central point represents the eternal Dharma. This directly means that this very eternal form of Dharma is also the basis of that form that is perpetually changeable and that gets impacted and directed by mind.

In normal life,the character,system and karma referred to as Dharma by the society are the result ofthose experiences ofmind that are changeable. The systemand rituals proposed by spiritual heads for use in this material life.

In normal life, the character, system and karma referred to as Dharma by the society are the result of those experiences of mind that are changeable. The system and rituals proposed by spiritual heads for use in this material life, that we refer to as 'Dharma' in social language, come under this very category. The decisions of any spiritual head may be imposed on this changeable world but they are neither everlasting nor eternal nor perpetual. Whether anybody agrees or not, all these systems proposed in the name of making life regular, controlled and disciplined and righteous. They are confined by place, time and circumstances and are helpful only to a very limited sense in the awakening of spiritual consciousness. When society is divided using these rituals and systems in the name of protecting discipline and Dharma, this ultimately gives rise to communal feeling. Communalism is the result of these very decisions, systems and discourses that have been assumed to be perpetual and eternal. Attempts have been made by self-proclaimed spiritual heads and their disciples to impose them on society and humanity. In short, it may be said that when 'existence' comes out of extrovert spiritual consciousness and reveals itself in outer world, it becomes communal. If we treat and recognise all the rules and regulations applicable for existence within the purview of mind as Dharma, then this form based on extrovert consciousness and mind also would get confined to place and time, get impacted by circumstances and keep on changing. However, this is certain that the Dharma existing within the purview of mind, though not perpetual, can surely be helpful to some extent for development of the existence of mind. The form of existence that is realised by mind sets up systems for its own development and creation. If those systems are given the identity of Dharma, all those systems that are being called 'Dharma' would certainly keep changing with time. However, there is also one another form of 'existence' that is not created by mind. There is also a part of existence that is not understood by mind and we may have to encroach upon the mind to get familiar with. That form of existence that we find by looking beyond our mind and senses can neither be mortal nor changeable.

If we treat and recognise all the rules and regulations applicable for existence within the purview of mind as Dharma, then this form based on extrovert consciousness and mind also would get confined to place.

Scientists may question if there is really an existence that is beyond our mind. Indian philosophy openly recognises that there is an existence beyond mind and this existence beyond mind is eternal, static and constant. However, science believes only on senses. It wants to find out everything through these senses. It is its compulsion to learn through the senses. However, science accepts that many of its systems and many of its decisions and inferences might have been different had there been any extra sense organ available to science. Today, science is only deliberating on the question whether it is possible to reach beyond the mind by trespassing the existing senses, whereas, it is well recognised by Indian philosophy that it is possible to go beyond the mind.

Indian philosophy believes that science may experience the existence beyond mind. In that case, science would have to also accept all the disciplines that have been prescribed for going beyond the existence of mind. In this context, Rajneesh has clearly written in his book 'Adhyatm Upanishad'–"It is the original discovery of India that existence can be perceived even without the mind. Science maintains that whatever is to be understood can be perceived with just the help of mind, Dharma claims that whatever is perceived through the mind is just passable. That is at most near the truth. Whatever is understood beyond mind only is truth, and the real understanding is possible only beyond mind."

It is possible that science may have an objection to this and it may say that real understanding is only that which can be proven in a laboratory. In a sense, this thinking is not incorrect for any scientist, but if he goes little deep he may even have to look at the apparatus used in the laboratory or the structure of the laboratory. Can science perform all the experiments in a single laboratory? Is nuclear fission possible in the laboratory of a chemist? It is clear that we need to create a laboratory as per the requirements of the knowledge that we wish to acquire. Is science capable of fabricating a laboratory the kind of which may be required to understand eternal truth? If at all science ever becomes able to fabricate such a laboratory, it would still be different from the laboratory that is created by mind. The laboratory created by the mind may be helpful to science to an extent, but if science has to understand the existence, it would have delve deeper into the levels of consciousness and would be courageous to leap into the unknown. Otherwise also, whatever science has discovered has been achieved only by leaping into the unknown. It is not possible to make a new discovery without leaping into the unknown.

It is possible that science may have an objection to this and it may say that real understanding is only that which can be proven in a laboratory.

Experience is always extremely personal and individualised. Once a person gains some experience, it is not possible to have exactly the same experience later even by the same person. It means that any experience cannot be repeated completely. And hence, experience or realisation cannot be ever passed on fully to any other person by means of words. All experiences in the domain of Dharma are extremely personal and individualised. The disciples of Jesus Christ would not have had the same experience and realisation that Jesus Christ might have had. It is not possible also. The disciples of Muhammad can never have the same experience and realisation that Muhammad would have had while exploring Dharma for the purpose of discovering supreme truth. The same thing can be said about those experiences of the saints and sages, the gist of which we find in the Upanishads. Readers or seekers would not get to know the real truth of those realisations of the Supreme Being that are expressed in words in Upanishads, by just reading and studying them. If anybody wants to know the truth of Upanishads, he would have to descend deep down, drown within, and get lost, just like our sages, to gain experience and realisation.

All experiences in the domain of Dharma are extremely personal and individualised. The disciples of Jesus Christ would not have had the same experience and realisation that Jesus.

The truth that is realised and understood by diving deep into introverted consciousness never gets divided. It is not possible that the truth of the Upanishads be different from the truth of Jesus Christ. It also is not possible that the truth of 'Dhammapad' be different from the truth of Upanishads. It is also not possible that the truth recorded in the verses of the Holy Quran be different from the truth of that supreme realisation that Hazarat Muhammad attained. It is the ultimate and supreme truth as understood by him, while entering the introverted consciousness in supreme silence. Whoever has understood truth must have plunged deep and then only, he would have reached the pinnacle of his realisation.

In the eyes of a scientist, there is no solid matter or physical matter and they are all only electrical energy as found after tests in laboratories. Similarly, as per spiritual consciousness found in the laboratories of the spiritual domain, all the visible things are just Param Chaitanya. Philosophy claims that everything is just a form of this Chaitanya and there is no existence separate from this Chaitanya. This existence of Chaitanya that is called the Supreme Being or Divinity is all pervading, everlasting, eternal and infinite and has its own discipline. This discipline is nothing else but its character only that is also dualism and even beyond dualism. This very character is the real identity of that 'Supreme Being' and this is the 'Dharma' of Param Chaitanya. This is the true 'Sanatana Dharma'. The Dharma of Supreme Being and its perpetuity, omniscience, everlastingness, completeness and wholeness and its immensity cannot be divided. The thing that is called Chaitanya by philosophy is referred to as energy or electricity by science. Scientists say that all matter is created by energy and energy can never be divided. There is no way to divide energy or electricity which keeps on flowing perpetually even if nobody is able to perceive it. This very perpetual flow of energy is its continuity and character and hence it is Dharma. There is no difference between this Dharma of energy and the Dharma of Chaitanya. Existence is only one, whether we call it electric energy or Chaitanya or Supreme Being. The name does not make any difference. Assigning a name would not alter the character of the Supreme Being. Though Chaitanya may not be assigned any name, we do assign a name for easy thinking or recognition. Otherwise also, while contemplating on this subject, while diving deep within, we reach a situation when all the names disappear. However, this is a stage beyond this world, even beyond Dharma. Nobody knows what lies beyond the perimeters of Dharma and the Supreme Being. In the sense of logic, if there is 'something', there must be a 'nonentity'. If there is infinity, there must be something beyond infinity also, but this logic looks more like prevarication than logic. This argument may not be a chicanery, but this can surely be called too much of an argument.

In the eyes of a scientist, there is no solid matter or physical matter and they are all only electrical energy as found after tests in laboratories. Similarly, as per spiritual consciousness found in the laboratories of the spiritual domain.

□

5
Complete Human

It is the desire of every human being to become a complete human being. Wherever imbalance exists in him should end. He wants to move from darkness to light, from incompleteness to completeness. He even wants to conquer death. Death makes a human being aware of his incompleteness, hence he is also afraid of death. What is birth? What is death? What is the Dharma of death? What is the Dharma of birth? He is a bit afraid to look deep into his mind to find out answers to these questions. However, this also is an eternal truth that without diving deep into the mind and without recognising his fundamental form, a man can neither remain balanced nor be complete nor conquer death. The name of that framework that contains the mystery of birth and death and secrets of becoming a complete man is 'Dharma'. These mysteries cannot be uncovered by means of collective programs. Hence, Dharma is an extremely personal consciousness. Awakening of this personal consciousness starts when the person starts conquering self-interest and self-ego. After reaching this stage, the seeker does not look for peace in outer self and this world rather he attempts to find mysteries of peace and poise in his inner self.

The unease visible in the context of society is only a result of the state of mind of the mankind. Our mindset determines the character of our society. We see the reflection of our own minds in our society. Whatever we see through our minds only become visible to us. The society may have a facet that may not be of interest for us. Even if that facet of society is presented in front of us, we prefer to remain ignorant about it. If the mind is restless, the society also would appear restless.

If the mind is anxious and agitated, society also would manifest anxiety and uneasiness only.

If the mind is filled with peace and happiness, even the greatest grief can be surmounted. However, we have to fill our inner self with happiness to conquer grief. Neither a complete man can be created nor can a man be made well-balanced without the transformation of inner self.

A one-sided psyche is not beneficial for society. This is correct that the entire world is a form of Bramha only and all inanimate and living things in this world are projections of that single Param Chaitanya only. But, this projection indicates two aspects. The first one is - whatever is outside is the perpetually changeable world, and the other one is whatever is in the inner self is the unabridged existence of self. Both of these are goals of Dharma. One is the encounter with the whole existence and the other is extinguishment of the ignorance of changeability. The obscurity of ignorance can be removed only by Dharma. That, which is not competent to remove that obscurity of ignorance cannot be called Dharma. The darkness in the inner self of a person is removed only by the consciousness that is gained in the functional form of Dharma. This consciousness is capable of providing peace and happiness to the mind. A well-balanced and complete personality may be developed with the help of this consciousness only. For balancing, we may have to look not only towards the outer world but also towards the inner world. A person would not be able to find peace and happiness, poise and completeness only in the outer world. He would have to take the help from both sides to attain poise or balance. While, on one side, he would have to correct his inner self, on the other side, he would need to keep working in the outer world also. However, how to conduct oneself in the outer world and what is the relationship between outer world and inner world - these subjects also fall in the purview of Dharma.

The darkness in the inner self of a person is removed only by the consciousness that is gained in the functional form of Dharma. This consciousness is capable of providing peace and happiness to the mind.

Those who think that one's personality may be made well-balanced and complete by fully renouncing outer world are under a misconception. Whatever is there in Nature, whatever and however is its existence - we need to accept the same in full and accept the same as-it-is; only after that the mysteries of balance and completeness can be uncovered. If anybody wants to find peace and balance inside caves in forests and mountains, fleeing away from the world i.e. external world, he would not be able to find them even there. Otherwise also, it's is not possible to renounce the world. Similarly, balance or poise is not the name of conquering mental instincts. Dharma does cover the art of transforming the instincts of mind, but conquering them is not linked to Dharma. Dharma is the name of the art that helps in connecting the mind to the consciousness of bliss. Until that state is attained and until mental instincts get directly linked to Param Chaitanya and that is realised, real happiness and real balance are not achieved. Discovery of balance and completeness is the subject matter of Dharma.

Dharma is the name of the art that helps in connecting the mind to the consciousness of bliss. Until that state is attained and until mental instincts get directly linked to Param Chaitanya.

Whatever human endeavours are there for attaining completeness and balance, they are called Dharma in colloquial language. If these endeavours are self-inspired i.e. they are born out of lack of arrogance, selflessness and motive of discovering consciousness of oneness, the duty bound karma created from it comes under the purview of Dharma. In Indian philosophy, this duty is called 'Purushartha'. Four *purusharthas* that find place in Indian culture are - *Dharma, artha, kama and moksha*. In the context of purushartha, Dharma refers to duty of a person towards his society, his family, his parents, his brother, her brother, towards parents, and a neighbour towards his neighbour. The importance of duty in the domain of Dharma is infinite.

Those who enter the domain of Dharma do not talk of rights, as they cannot talk of rights at all. The moment they talk of rights, they are filled with self-interest and arrogance, whereas, Dharma makes us free from arrogance and self-interest. Anything that is filled with self-interest and arrogance cannot be called Dharma. The spirit of self-interest and arrogance is against the consciousness of that colossal and supreme Chaitanya who has the characteristics of supreme oneness, bliss and completeness. The existence of Dharma is linked to duty-centred consciousness. When we move further ahead to explore duty, we find Society Dharma, Business Dharma, Human Dharma, Ancestry Dharma, Age Dharma and similarly, whatever in this world comes in contact with us, the duty towards it becomes a part of our Dharma. This is the mystery of Dharma in the context of external world. Those who understand this mystery enter the process of becoming a complete man. Those who do not understand this mystery are able to become neither balanced nor complete. To understand this mystery, a person would have to first understand his reality by getting into his inner consciousness. Only after understanding oneself fully, the reality of the existence that appears to be separate can be understood. Why that 'Supreme Oneness' that is whole appears separate? There is no straight answer to this. The only thing that can be said is that this is his magnanimity. Actually, there is no second entity in this world at all. Just 'He, the one' exists. Sages have expressed this very fact as 'एकोब्रह्म द्वितियोनास्ति' (*'ekobramha dvitiyonaasti'*). This is that knowledge that helps in understanding Chaitanya. This very consciousness helps in understanding the whole. This is that consciousness which is helpful in all respects to lead a person towards completeness. This awakening of consciousness only helps us in moving towards balance and completeness. And this very consciousness of awakening is the divinity of a person and this divinity is his real duty and hence his Dharma also.

Those who do not understand this mystery are able to become neither balanced nor complete. To understand this mystery,a person would have to first understand his reality by getting into his inner consciousness.

There is nobody who does not want to be complete and balanced and who does not have the desire to enjoy happiness and pleasure; but his desire does not get fulfilled. Mankind has crossed many stages during the course of his ideological journey. He has achieved many heights and has also suffered setbacks sometimes, but this journey of development is still incomplete. This journey is still continuing and would continue until mankind finds the fundamental essence of his existence.

Here, a question may also be raised to ascertain where is the evidence to confirm that the mankind is slowly developing. There can be only one evidence for it - whether the person who is striving for self-development has undergone any change in his inner self? This creation is a mixture of three basic components - *sattva, raja and tama*. 'What is *tamas*?' is a different question. But this tamas is a reality. Otherwise, the main reason for this tamas is ignorance. Before we look for the answer to the question 'Why there is ignorance?' we should understand that if there were no ignorance, there could not have been disquiet, fight, aberration and grief. Tamas is there as ignorance is there, and that's why there are conflicts, perturbation and restlessness. That's also why there is incompleteness and unbalance in a person. Existence of incompleteness and disbalance in a person is the sign of tamas filled in him. If tamas is to be conquered, first of all he will have to look towards his own character. An average person does not look towards himself, instead he explores external society to seek reasons of all his problems. However, the real reason for an affliction lies within the person and not in the society. Society may help in aggravating a disease or making it more complicated. Furthermore, the main germs of the disease reside not in the society but in the person himself. Hence, the person would have to first of all cleanse his inner self. A person with inner-self filled with tamas and barbarity, despite having secured unlimited material prosperity, would never be able to have the capability to enjoy this prosperity happily. This is the basic reason that the person is not able to enjoy happily all that he has and runs after the things that he does not have. This is mental imbalance. Dharma is the science that creates the means for clearing the darkness of the inner self and makes it explicit as to which direction the person needs to direct the flow of consciousness to improve his personality. There is no meaning to

That's also why there is incompleteness and unbalance in a person. Existence of incompleteness and disbalance in a person is the sign of tamas filled in him.

the prosperity in outer world if the inner-self continues to be poor. And there is no meaning to the light in outer world if the inner-self is filled with darkness.

It is well recognised that lakhs of years ago, man was only an animal. Slowly he evolved from animal to human. This journey of development from animal to human is still incomplete. Man has to become a complete man and man would become a complete man only when he would be able to remove the impurity within himself. Lust, rage, attachment, food, sleep, fear and sex are Dharma for animals also. A man's Dharma must be certainly something more than that, must be something special. Intelligence is available with animals also; they even have memory. Some of the qualities like - kindness, compassion, feeling of welfare for all, tolerance, magnanimity, feeling of self-sacrifice are prevalent more in humans than in animals. The more a person's inner-self is filled with these excellent values, the more we may treat him as relatively better developed. In the beginning, there was no difference other than body structure between undeveloped human being and an animal. The development-journey from an undeveloped human being to a complete human being i.e. a human being who has attained completeness is, in the words of Rishi Aurobindo, a journey towards divinity. A properly developed human being only would ultimately be a complete human being. This very divinity is the Dharma of mankind. There is a rule for attaining this divinity, and the first step of that rule is development of the will power of self. To attain divinity, the person must have thirst and inquisitiveness of such a level that he is ready to give his entire life force to fulfill it. This only is the test of his commitments. When a person moves ahead on the path of divinity with full commitment, he may be said to be proceeding towards becoming a complete man.

It is well recognised that lakhs of years ago, man was only an animal. Slowly he evolved from animal to human. This journey of development from animal to human is still incomplete.

Material progress is certainly a big achievement of mankind. Science has a big contribution in this material progress. The intelligence that humans possess also has contributed a lot in this material progress. The irony is that the same intelligence has been used by mankind to accumulate instruments for destruction of not only themselves but everybody. Can a person, who has knowingly accumulated instruments of mass destruction, be called balanced? An unbalanced person cannot be accepted as a developed person. A person who is pushing himself as well as the entire mankind to death - can we call such a person a complete human? This is such an eternal question that even asking a person today to answer it makes him perturbed and he tries to evade the question; but this escapist attitude is not going to serve anything. It is unfortunate that the man in today's world is becoming more escapist than going deeper into his problems. His moral conduct has become like that of an ostrich. If we examine this ostrich-like conduct or pigeon-like conduct of a man against criteria in the context of his development-journey, it will be apparent that the man has made very insignificant development on the level of his inner-self and the claims of his development are just pretensions. It is the need of the hour to save mankind from this hypocrisy and divert him towards finding and understanding those mysteries that would help him become a complete man in the real sense.

Material progress is certainly a big achievement of mankind. Science has a big contribution in this material progress. The intelligence that humans possess also has contributed a lot in this material progress.

Dharma does not mobilise the means of destruction of mankind. It only mobilises means of thorough development of mankind; it is the main instrument for his all-round and balanced development. Dharma means all round development- not only self-development but also the development of the entire living world and entire Nature. As the thinking of our Indian philosophers is 'सर्व भूत हिते रत:' a true righteous person does not care for his self-interests. Instead, he embraces the feeling of welfare for all in his life. The feeling of welfare for all is not an item of demonstration. If ever a person attempts to demonstrate his feeling of welfare for all, he would be, in a way, marching on the path of pretence only. Demonstration of the feeling of welfare for all just means augmentation of self-interest and development of arrogance. A person, who is busy in development of his arrogance and is looking for contentment in his arrogance, can never become one doing common good in real sense. Such a person would be ultimately selfish, intransigent, narrow-minded and unrighteous. This is the reason that even the persons claiming to be following the path of righteousness are not able to become good for all due to their arrogance. The more a person nourishes his arrogance the more he becomes communal. In the real sense, communalism is another form of unrighteousness. Nobody can ever become a complete man by following the path of communalism. The path of communalism can never be the path to divinity. A person can uncover neither the mysteries of himself nor the mysteries of Dharma by following this path. When a person links his arrogance and self-interest to rituals and other religious ceremonies and starts giving them maximum importance, he goes astray all the more. This disorientation is only plaguing the world to a great extent today. It is the reason for most of the perversions in mankind and is the biggest obstacle in the path of making a man complete.

A person, who is busy in development of his arrogance and is looking for contentment in his arrogance, can never become one doing common good in real sense.

It is essential to rekindle the fire within, to correct this loss of sense of direction. We cannot rekindle the fire within with the help of flame provided by others. We will have to discover the flame ourselves. We will have to rekindle our fire on our own. This is what Mahatma Buddha also used to say. The last advice that he gave to his greatest disciple Anand at the time of his death was 'अप्प दीप्पो भव' ('appa deepo bhava), that means - be your own lamp and do not cast your life into the mould of definitions provided by others. Increase the intensity of your inquisitiveness on your own and reach the extremity that is possible by your senses with the help of your experiences. These very experiences ultimately take us beyond the senses where realisation starts. Spiritual realisation cannot be expressed in words. We can constrain with words only those things that come in contact with our senses. The realisation that comes out of our soul and that grows from the energy of our soul cannot be expressed in words. There is no feeling of dualism at all in this realisation and when there is no feeling of dualism, where is the question of 'I' and 'You'? This contains the ultimate realisation and the ultimate realisation is unique. In other words, when the ultimate realisation occurs, all differences among known, knowable and knowledge disappear. The soul uncovers its mysteries only in front of those who efface themselves. He who effaces himself goes beyond death. Only he who effaces himself tastes *amrit*. Only that person can enjoy *amrit* who breaches even the consciousness of being human. Dharma after all is the ultimate mystery. The science of Dharma explains to us the system of being supernatural. Its development orients us towards being complete human beings, and that's why it is said that Dharma is an extremely personal realisation. This ultimate personal realisation is one that becomes universal, everlasting and ubiquitous. Under such moments of realisation, the feeling of dualism disappears and even the feeling of non-duality is lost, as the existence of 'I' cannot be a part of that realisation where 'I' has been completely lost.

Spiritual realisation cannot be expressed in words. We can constrain with words only those things that come in contact with our senses. The realisation that comes out of our soul and that grows from the energy of our soul.

This is not correct to say that only one path is prescribed for the process of divinity of a person. This process of divinity is extremely personal. There are as many ways as there are living beings. This arrangement may be expressed in another way also - the entire creation would ultimately attain supreme divineness only with the process of continuous development. The supreme divineness that we may call Param Chaitanya or even Supreme Being is the source of creation of this entire universe. Further, this universe would ultimately get merged with it. The truth is that one who is born is sure to die. But the mystery of this life and death is circular. We will have to dive very deep into our inner-self to understand this. We will have to discipline our consciousness in a specific way. This very supreme discipline of personal consciousness creates the steps towards divinity.

One question may be raised here - why should the materialistic man of today go for divinity? What benefits is he going to get from this divinity? Can he attain prosperity with this divinity? Can this divinity provide food to him? Can this help in removing poverty? Can this help in providing education to people and can this provide other material facilities? All these questions are meaningless. They are meaningless because Dharma or divinity does not have any conflict with them. Divinity cannot at all have any conflict with materialism, as material prosperity is also a part of the Supreme Being only. Is material prosperity not a part of the whole or totality? It is very much recognised that whatever is there in this creation is a form entirely of Param Chaitanya only. Hence, prosperity also cannot be separate from Param Chaitanya. Divinity means that the person should recognise his true self by exploring his inner-self so that his misconceptions, perturbations, confusions and ignorance may get removed. A restless and perturbed person cannot attain prosperity properly and he is not able to enjoy properly whatever little prosperity he attains. Hence, divinity does not have any conflict with material prosperity.

One question may be raised here - why should the materialistic man of today go for divinity? What benefits is he going to get from this divinity? Can he attain prosperity with this divinity? Can this divinity provide food to him?

The truth is that the word conflict itself disappears under the consciousness of divinity. The consciousness of divinity is only the consciousness that takes a person towards the supreme oneness. This supreme oneness only makes one realise the existence of non-dualism. The eternity of non-dualism and realisation of its existence only would ultimately provide mankind, the consciousness and all the instruments that would help him attain completeness. Completeness means that the man is ready to perform all his duties staying in his own character. It does not have any conflict with karma; rather its conflict is with that consciousness that makes a person miserable, incomplete and unhappy. The situation of divisions and differences that exists in human society today because of incompleteness is the source of all the discords prevalent in the world. These very discords generate disturbances at all levels. They prevent real development of consciousness of peace, cordiality, friendship, love and brotherhood in inner-self. The virtues imposed from outside give rise to hypocrisy only; they do not find out any real solution to any of the problems faced by mankind. A correct and permanent solution to a problem can be found only when the inner-self is transformed. This very transformation of the inner-self is the real purpose of the Dharma of human being. This transformation of the inner-self is not impossible. This would however be possible only when a person abandons his ignorance. His consciousness remains forever under the feeling that only one Chaitanya is all pervading. Whatever is happening, is visible, is being experienced and is being expressed in thoughts, are all aimed towards removal of ignorance. Nobody can stop the attempts or the process of removal of ignorance or the process of moving from incompleteness to completeness. If however, one is able to cooperate in the process consciously, attaining completeness may become still simpler and easier.

If however, one is able to cooperate in the process consciously, attaining completeness may become still simpler and easier.

The meaning and purpose of Dharma is to move ahead consciously for attaining completeness. This is not impossible; but this requires one to go through a discipline. This is not only the discipline of external senses, but also the discipline of the inner-self. One has to be careful though to understand that suppression of senses cannot be called discipline. Instead of suppressing the senses, we should aim to develop such a consciousness that is born out of the feeling of supreme oneness and introspection. Once our inner-self understands and feels the reality of the self and its existence, then it ceases to be slave to the senses, instead, the senses of such a person remain under his discipline automatically. This can also be expressed in other words that 'discipline of the senses' becomes the character of such an introvert and conscious person.

□

6

Dharmachakra Pravartanaay

Primitive humans possibly used prayers and worship to fight and calm down natural calamities and, treating the mysteries of natural forces as divine forces. They started humanising their characters, created idols of gods and goddesses, painted their pictures and explored options to please them. The humans gave these very prayers, worship and rituals the name of Dharma and treated this Dharma as the means for their prosperity and happiness. Humankind underwent further development and they learnt to be introvert and attempted to uncover their own mysteries. They tried to find out if there was any fundamental relation between themselves and Nature. This process of introverted contemplation generated new and wonderful dimensions to life. The reward that has been ultimately achieved after these thinking, contemplation and churning till now is great. It is the realisation of eternity, timelessness, wholeness, omnisciency and infiniteness of 'Param Chaitanya'. In this spiritualty only, thinking and meditating humans could see 'Rit Dharma'. There have been such super humans also who not only understood the existence of 'Rit Dharma' but also lived their life according to those beliefs. The knowledge and experiences that they provided to the mankind by removing credibility gaps were referred by them as 'Dharma'. These super humans treated Dharma as an action and not just a name. They selected a symbol to represent this divine thinking- they called it as *'Dharmachakra'*.

It is the quality of Chaitanya to appear as eternally flowing. This Chaitanya cannot be understood fully, but its partial realisation can be had with meditation using the process of 'नेति-नेति' ('neti neti') i.e. 'not this, not this'. Here, meditation does not mean becoming inanimate or sitting continuously at one place. Meditation means going ahead with one's karma with realisation of all pervading Chaitanya, performing all karma remaining under consciousness of supreme oneness. And this is also a fact that when this state of meditation is achieved after transformation of inner-self, the karma is performed for the benefit of all. There is one more process to know, understand and realise Chaitanya. That is, whatever comes in a person's contact, his experiences and his thoughts, treat all those things as the forms of Chaitanya. One can attain the realisation of supreme oneness through both the processes and both come under the purview of 'Rit Dharma'.

One has to move ahead avoiding any attachment with whatever is experienced and whatever is seen in the process of 'नेति-नेति', treating them as '*this is not the truth*'. Mankind would have to move ahead in search of truth, without any stop, without any pause, 'चरैवेति चरैवेति' ('charaiveti charaiveti') i.e. 'move on, move on'. *'Dharmachakra'* is the symbol of this very intensive search for truth. Rarely is anybody able to make an intensive search for truth. Firstly, the desire to start the search itself is developed with much difficulty. If at all, the desire is developed, the self-interest and arrogance of senses-dominant extrovert life create innumerable hurdles. *'Dharmachakra'* keeps on moving ahead towards its destination ignoring all these hurdles completely. There is no pause or rest even for a moment in the mentality of this *'Dharmachakra'*. *'Dharmachakra'* is not only a symbol of perpetual motion; it is not a normal motion; it is progress, only perpetual progress, perpetual development and perpetual upliftment.

'Dharmachakra' is the symbol ofthis very intensive search for truth. Rarely is anybody able to make an intensive search for truth. Firstly, the desire to start the search itselfis developed with much difficulty.

There are many forms of consciousness and accumulation and cohesion of all those forms only is 'Param Chaitanya'. Why Param Chaitanya expresses itself in innumerable or infinite forms i.e. why this 'whole' appears to be fragmented in its extroverted existence - there is no way to find an answer to this question. A part can never have complete understanding of the existence of the whole; but this also is a supreme truth that the part also is a piece of the whole only. The part may not have memory of this status, but just this loss of memory would not change that fact, that truth. The very remedy to this amnesia is 'Rit Dharma'. And this is the purpose of *'Dharmachakra'*. *'Dharmachakra'* is the symbol of that progress which helps mankind to move ahead towards attainment of completeness. *'Dharmachakra'* is not only a symbol of motion. A motion may even be in opposite direction i.e. towards decline. However, in the context of *'Dharmachakra'*, intention is the only perpetual development, that also only perpetual development for welfare and benefit to all - this again is the real intention of Dharma. Any intention other than this is not even admissible as the very meaning of 'Dharma' is 'सर्वभूतहिते रतः' (*'sarvabhoot hite ratah'*) i.e. welfare for all creatures, inanimate and living objects and all known and unknown. 'Dharma' is in all forms, a divine truth and that which is divine truth would be always having creativity and intention of welfare and happiness only. 'Divine' truth is not a symbol of narrow-mindedness and self-interest; rather it is bearer of the idea of 'complete welfare', 'complete development' and 'supreme oneness'.

'Dharma' is in all forms, a divine truth and that which is divine truth would be always having creativity and intention of welfare and happiness only. 'Divine' truth is not a symbol of narrow-mindedness and self-interest.

The idea of complete welfare, development and supreme oneness is actually the indication of that state of dualism where there would be welfare and development for all. In such circumstances, a situation and environment would be created for the development of solidarity and family values. However, in this welfare-centric development journey, none would do anything that he would have rejected, if done to him under the same circumstances. The principle is - 'आत्मनः प्रतिकूलानि परेषां न समाचारेत' (*'aatmanah pratikoolani pareshan na samaacharet'*) i.e. the behaviour that appears unfavourable to self is prohibited. The very essence of Dharma in our life is this. Anything opposite to it is immoral and inauspicious.

There cannot be any better thinking than *'Dharmachakra'* for the advancement of mankind. Possibly, this was the reason that, immediately after independence, the mission statement, the goal or the intention that the helmsmen of India and architects of our constitution approved for Indian parliament was - *'Dharmachakra Pravartanaay'* (धर्मचक्र प्रवर्तनाय). This intention of the parliament is embedded in golden letters behind the chair of speaker so that, every moment, this reminds every politician sitting in the hall, of the mission, goal and aim. One of the meanings of this cherished goal of the parliament is also that this would be the goal of Indian politics. Every parliamentarian would dedicate himself to uphold *'Dharmachakra',* would remain alert towards it. He would not do or say anything that goes against feeling of purity and feeling of welfare for all enshrined in the *'Dharmachakra'.* However, did it really happen? Is Indian politics *'Dharmachakra Pravartanaay'* i.e. aimed to enforce Dharmachakra, in real sense? Has the Indian parliament been successful in the enforcement of *'Dharmachakra'?* Is the Indian parliament concerned about 'धर्मचक्र प्रवर्तन' (*'Dharmachakra Pravartan)'* i.e. enforcement of *'Dharmachakra'.* Is the body really committed and dedicated towards it? There is not one but many such questions that the people of India may ask their politicians and their parliamentarians. Unfortunately, Indian voters, Indian people do not enforce accountability by their representatives and specially their parliamentarians. This is the reason that the dreams of architects of constitution are getting shattered one by one and the things that are taking shape are opportunism, partiality, political corruption, criminalisation, exploitation and injustice.

The helmsmen of India were never of the view that 'Dharmachakra Pravartanaay' was intended only for the parliament or politics. They also would not have thought that the symbol of 'Dharmachakra'.

The helmsmen of India were never of the view that *'Dharmachakra Pravartanaay'* was intended only for the parliament or politics. They also would not have thought that the symbol of *'Dharmachakra'* would remain just as a fantasy or become a symbol of hypocrisy. The truth is that the proclamation of *'Dharmachakra Pravartanaay'* was accepted as a national proclamation. The character and the life-style of entire nation, society and each and every citizen of the country should be '*Dharmachakra Pravartanaay*' - that was the real intention. That which is not the goal of nation, that which is not the aim of the people of country - how can they be made goal and aim of the parliament? But it has been unfortunate, and that is still continuing, that the people of this country were never motivated towards the spirit of '*Dharmachakra*'. Though '*Dharmachakra Pravartanaay*' has been the principle of the nation and the parliament, no attempt was at all made after independence to make this principle a part of the national lifestyle. As also, create an environment for this principle to take the shape of national consciousness. Another bitter truth is that, 'attempts are being made to discourage or destroy whatever casual and occasional belief is found towards the proclamation of *Dharmachakra*'. This is the biggest misfortune for India and this is the biggest betrayal of the nation. And especially those who belong to politics are committing this betrayal.

It has now become necessary to find out the prime reasons of the current indifference and disbeliefof parliamentarians and Indian politics towards that grand sentence that is embossed in golden letters.

It has now become necessary to find out the prime reasons of the current indifference and disbelief of parliamentarians and Indian politics towards that grand sentence that is embossed in golden letters above the seat of Lok Sabha speaker. The nation would have to contemplate as to why Indian politics is now beset with a sense of indifference towards this proclamation that they had accepted as prime cornerstone of their consciousness and strength. The nation would certainly introspect on this issue someday but the first responsibility of contemplation on the issue lies with the speaker of Lok Sabha, the prime minister of India, the council of ministers and the leader of opposition in the parliament. What would the nation do if these current fortune-makers of the country forget their duties? How can the general people of society become conscious of the national ideals if even political power and administration of the country lose sight of their duties?

This is a very big irony in itself that proclamation of '*Dharmachakra Pravartanaay*' has been imprinted in the parliament in golden letters but none of the governments or political parties has ever explained its meaning to their parliamentarians. These parliamentarians do not even know how and what kind of inspiration is expected to be derived from this national proclamation. Most of the parliamentarians are even not aware if they have any responsibility towards this great proclamation and desire. Till date, no write-up has been created by the Indian government or by the parliament or by parliament secretariat that could explain the expectations enshrined in '*Dharmachakra Pravartanaay*'. What is the role of '*Dharmachakra*' in national development - this is not officially documented anywhere. In short, Indian parliament is completely ignorant of and also blind to the great national proclamation, desire and goal.

One misconception that politicians are nourishing because of their own self-interests and the self-interests of priestism, is that there are many Dharmas and that's why they do not speak anything on this subject. Any comment on this subject would be a disregard of the ideals of democracy and detrimental to public confidence. There seems to be no possibility of this misconception of politicians being removed in the near future, as publicising Dharma in multiple forms helps them create vote banks and increases the possibility of political use of public hysteria. The situation is quite grave and there is also a serious danger for humanity. This fallacious interpretation of 'Dharma' and related thinking has made mankind orthodox, fanatical and conservative and hence its repudiation has become unavoidable. However, who would do that repudiation and how? How to go for correction when current politicians are not ready to face and understand the truth? How to remove the blindfolds? Those blindfolds tied by their own hands would have to be removed by them only; then only they would get their sight back. Escapism is not going to help anyway. Sooner or later,

One misconception that politicians are nourishing because of their own self-interests and the self-interests of priestism, is that there are many Dharmas and that's why they do not speak anything on this subject.

politicians would have to understand that there is no place for multiplicity in 'Dharma' as that is only internal realisation and a process of internal transformation. Dharma is definitely not an ideology or discipline. There is no place for community, separation and division in this supreme knowledge. Knowledge cannot be acquired only by debates; truth can be found slowly by internal contemplation, cogitation and meditation. Until truth comes to politics, it is not possible to have peace in the world. Untruth, using various means and manipulations, would only give rise to discrimination, bloodshed, wars and exploitation. That is its character.

It's not that scriptures are useless. It's also not correct to say that the thoughts of great persons and their contemplations are inauspicious. The point to be thought over and understood is- what was the intention of the great men like Mahavira, Buddha and Jesus? The intention of these great saints was - 'you should change', 'a person's inner-self should be transformed'. Whatever core contemplation these great men went through was only intended to ensure that the man removed the feeling of discrimination from his inner-self and started loving all, treating them as his own forms in real sense, and created an atmosphere of welfare for all. It was the due to the intention of those great men that mankind got rid of their ignorance, arrogance and inertia. Later, the then disciples of these great men, and those existing today, created sects for their own self-interest, established camps of disparity and encouraged their own ego by treating themselves superior. This growing arrogance made these disciples still more narrow-minded, conservative and violent. Now the situation is quite complicated, but where is the fault of Dharma in all this? Where is the fault of those great saints in all this? How can spiritual consciousness be held offender or accused for the degeneration that is observed now?

It was the due to the intention ofthose great men that mankind got rid oftheir ignorance, arrogance and inertia. Later,the then disciples ofthese great men,and those existing today, created sects for their own self.

The scriptures suggest - examine whatever is written there, adopt them in your life and transform your inner-self. The scriptures provide all kinds of tips and signals in the context of the truth of life. Their aim is to make us march ahead until completeness is achieved. The goal is also to make us remove all divisions, end all hatred, keep moving ahead and keep trying for transformation of inner-self. In reality this is the 'Rit Dharma' and this is the ideal of '*Dharmachakra*'. We cannot define 'Dharma' by means of scriptures, as Dharma is a self-realisation. To attain 'righteousness', to understand it is an eternal transformation. Here, 'to understand' means 'to become'. This very craving for 'to become' encourages us to move ahead and transform ourselves.

Today, it has become very necessary to comprehensively interpret the proclamation and mission statement of '*Dharmachakra Pravartanaay*' that the Indian parliament accepted for itself. 'Dharma' is now being referred to in the parliament in a very conservative way. The ignorance of parliamentarians in respect of the word 'Dharma' has crossed all limits. 'Dharma' and 'Religion' and 'Mazahab' are not synonyms. Though almost all Presidents have repeated the same thing many times in their addresses, this misconception has not gone. Dr. Radhakrishnan even presented a comprehensive interpretation of the word 'Dharma' many times, but his words also were ignored. Similarly, President Dr. Shankar Dayal Sharma also made comprehensive interpretation of the word 'Dharma' many times and accepted it as separate from 'Religion. However, it is strange that the Indian Parliament has been openly disregarding these interpretations and thoughts presented by the Presidents and it is doing so even today. It appears that the average parliamentarian of India wants to knowingly remain attached to his mistake and misconception. Every parliamentarian must at least know the meaning of that great statement '*Dharmachakra Pravartanaay*'. This is the responsibility of Lok Sabha Speaker and the Prime Minister to find a suitable remedy to this blemish existing for a long time. '*Dharmachakra*' signifies the moving nature of Dharma. 'Chakra' is the symbol of motion and in spiritual consciousness this 'chakra' means that

> *The scriptures provide all kinds of tips and signals in the context of the truth of life. Their aim is to make us march ahead until completeness is achieved. The goal is also to make us remove all divisions, end all hatred.*

motion which is capable of removing ignorance, internal darkness and separation. The fundamental aim of the symbol of 'chakra' is to ensure end of injustice and protection of the oppressed. The idols of gods and goddesses created as symbols in Hindu consciousness, all have chakra in their hands. This chakra is used to destroy untruth and injustice. If we try to define *'Dharmachakra'* in this context, it may also mean that form of Dharma that is capable of putting an end to injustice, exploitation, ignorance and untruth. If injustice, exploitation, ignorance and untruth cannot be removed by means of Dharma, that Dharma would be called *'Adharma'* only.

The first part of the great statement *'Dharmachakra Pravartanaay'* is *'Dharma'* and the second part is *'Pravartanaay'*. 'Pravartan' means management, attitude, encouragement, enforcement, progress, commencement and adoption. The core of the word 'pravartan' is 'vartan' and 'pra' has been used only as a prefix. The prefix 'pra' means prosperity, movement, and behaviour. The word 'vartan' becomes very strong with the prefix 'pra' and it then represents management for progress and prosperity of the highest order. Hence, *'Dharmachakra Pravartanaay'* literally is derived as 'development-oriented management', growth in prosperity, initiation of the development process, commitment to welfare, all using Dharma. However, this literal interpretation would not help anybody - neither Dharma not the parliament. Hence, it would be appropriate for the parliament to go into the basic sentiment of this proclamation and bless the nation and give direction to it. The proclamation of *'Dharmachakra Pravartanaay'* would have to be understood in its appropriate and deeper perspective, in the context of common good and idea of welfare for all. This would be possible only when we separate our national consciousness from Western ideology and values. In the context of the word 'Dharma', we would have to get ourselves rid of Western values and interpretations; only then the darkness would disappear.

> *'Chakra' is the symbol of motion and in spiritual consciousness this 'chakra' means that motion which is capable of removing ignorance, internal darkness and separation.*
> *This chakra is used to destroy untruth and injustice.*

□

7

Dharmo Rakshati Rakshitah

Justice is Dharma and Dharma is justice. In a temporal sense, justice means righteous karma. Whatever karma is there in life that is unrighteous would be called injustice only and we may also call it exploitation and adharma. Adharma comes under the class of a crime and any unrighteous karma is a sin as well as a perversion that becomes the reason for the downfall of mankind and society. Hence, if prosperity is to be attained for society and progress is to be ensured for the mankind, they would have to be judicious in their deeds.

What is judicious karma, what is akarma, what is vikarma, what is Dharma, what is adharma - all these are certainly philosophical subjects but they are also linked to worldly life. Honesty and idealism are at the core of a righteous karma. That only is justice as well as Dharma. The righteous karma is value-centric and not person-centric. It may be correct that righteous karmas are connected to place, time and circumstances. Though such karmas are linked to the present, they are also connected to the greatest traditions of the past. Justice is definitely meant for the present. In the context of justice i.e. Dharma, present has the maximum importance and must be having at least some base. The structure of the base of the present cannot be created out of nothing. Thus, present also connects to previously-professed best values, traditions and ideals to make itself creditable. The present has the right to review previously tested traditions on the basis of rationality and to use rationality as a criterion for it. Rationality develops only when a person gets rid of self-interest, arrogance and attachment. When a person's rationality gets linked to self-interest, arrogance and attachment, it becomes polluted.

With a polluted rationality, Dharma cannot be protected. Dharma here means neither any rituals nor any majahab. Dharma here refers to common good and welfare for all. Such a karma that is good for all living beings and helps in overall development, encompassing all in this creation, inanimate or animate. When this feeling is established, then only is Dharma expressed in completeness, in real terms.

Dharma in its pure form is the signifier of the Whole. It is not only truth but also truth-centred development. Indian philosophers have termed Dharma as *'janaardan'* i.e. one who is invoked by all people for success and liberation, and have worshiped it treating it even as *'paramatma'*. In its pure form, Dharma is not time-bound, but in its worldly form i.e. after coming into temporal consciousness, it becomes time-bound. Being time-bound means respect for place, time and circumstances. When truth wants to express itself with due respect to place, time and circumstances, it falls back upon Dharma only. Whether truth is actually being expressed or not, its proof and confirmation depends on the creativity of karma and common good resulting from it. This process of common good and creativity can never be dependent on adharma. Wherever there is adharma or injustice, the feeling of common good can never get developed. When consciousness is based on Dharma, devoid of adharma, injustice, exploitation and attraction, the consciousness of common good, welfare, positivity, joy and overall development would take shape.

Whether truth is actually being expressed or not, its proof and confirmation depends on the creativity of karma and common good resulting from it. This process of common good and creativity can never be dependent on adharma.

One more important fact here is that the conception of Dharma as a form of the whole or non-dual is unimaginably colossal and it cannot be expressed in words; but when this colossal form comes down to temporal life, Dharma easily accepts the constraints of justice to express itself. This is why justice has been treated as the real epitome of Dharma and it would be always respectable, known as the best expression of divinity. In the context of justice, the architects of the Indian constitution have given maximum importance to Dharma in governance. The grand statement that the architects of constitution accepted as national proclamation in the context of justice is धर्मो रक्षति रक्षितः (*'Dharmo Rakshati Rakshitah'*). This statement, taken from *'Manusmriti'*, is the pillar of Indian judiciary. It simply means that Dharma would protect only those who protect Dharma. This also means that protection of Dharma only would help protect humanity. Protection of humanity means the prosperity of human beings in general, development of all living beings and welfare for all. Indian philosophers never treated Dharma with a narrow-minded view and connected it with the broadest possible consciousness in worldly life. According to Indian philosophers, where there is Dharma, there can never be discrimination. Even injustice is not possible there, just as where there is light, there can never be darkness. Dharma is light and even the deepest darkness disappears in its presence. The feelings of exploitation, injustice and anarchy disappear in the presence of Dharma; but Dharma would reside only where duty-bound karma or righteous karma is given maximum importance.

Indian philosophers never treated Dharma with a narrow-minded view and connected it with the broadest possible consciousness in worldly life. According to Indian philosophers,where there is Dharma,there can never be discrimination.

Detailed interpretations for justice and Dharma are provided in 12th to 15th shlokas of 8th chapter in Manusmriti. The portion that the architects of our constitution have selected as the great statement for the Supreme Court is the last part of the first line of 15th shloka. The entire shloka is as under:

"धर्म एव हतो हन्ति धर्मो रक्षति रक्षितः ।
तस्माद्धर्मो न हन्तव्यो मा नो धर्मो हतोऽवधीत् ।"

The literal meaning of the first line of above shloka is 'Dharma destroys those who destroy Dharma and when Dharma is protected, Dharma protects the protectors.' The meaning of this shloka is nice as this is the essence of justice, the duty of judiciary and also the duty of a nation and a society. Whenever Dharma is destroyed or damaged by any society, individual, community, organisation or association, the demolishers are also destroyed in the process. In fact, he who does not connect to Dharma is destroyed by Dharma. This also has a meaning that people who follow the path of Adharma can never attain physical, material and spiritual development at all. The path of Adharma means the path of injustice, the path of degeneration. Adharma means corruption, unrighteous karma. When unrighteous karma is performed knowingly, that karma becomes a crime and that in turn, destroys affluence, prosperity, name and fame. In the context of judiciary, this can be said that a judgement against duty-bound karma not only results in degeneration of the institution of judiciary. In fact, the judgement that is against duty-bound karma or against Dharma does not even get recognition from the general public. And the public ultimately destroy the judgement that is not acceptable to them. The public is all-powerful and preserver of world, hence the decision of Dharma and Adharma have to be taken only by accepting the spirit of common welfare and common good. That only which entails common good and development for all is Dharma and justice. Dharma should not be destroyed as its destruction results in destruction of nation.

According to Indian philosophy,Dharma is such a matter that is linked to a person even after death and does not get destroyed even after destruction ofthe body. Indian philosophers believe that every person should keepusing his body and move ahead.

According to Indian philosophy, Dharma is such a matter that is linked to a person even after death and does not get destroyed even after destruction of the body. Indian philosophers believe that every person should keep using his body and move ahead on his path of Dharma. When a person, while still in his body, follows the path of Dharma, he attains name, fame and prosperity. Name and fame is retained even after destruction of body, and whatever is retained after death is the real wealth of a person. The judiciary also would be able to attain name and fame only when it performs righteous karma i.e. it fulfills its duties in all circumstances. A judiciary that is ready to bow in front of power or any other pressure actually follows the path of Adharma. Whenever that happens, not only the judiciary but the power also has to face dishonour. For a democracy, this dishonour is the same as death.

In today's society, nobody can protect his duty-bound karma just on his own. In present times, a person needs the support of judiciary more than the support of power or administration, to follow the unhindered path of duty-bound karma. The demoniac elements or the criminal elements present in a society are the biggest hurdles in the path of duty-bound karma. Judiciary has the main responsibility for controlling those elements and destroying them. The society that is not bound by this duty-bound karma cannot attain majesty and prosperity; there can never be peace there. Only corruption breeds in such a society. Justice can be used to keep both society and power under discipline. This is the Dharma of judiciary to ensure that every section of the society i.e. every person of the nation follows his duty-bound karma in all respects. The word Dharma in the phrase 'धर्मो रक्षति रक्षितः' ('*Dharmo Rakshati Rakshitah*') actually refers to duty-bound karma only. This duty-bound karma is the sole criterion for a person to be righteous. Neither the rituals nor the system of worship nor the principles scripted in religious books can become criteria for righteousness of any person, class or society. Prayers, worships, offers and chants also do not provide any indication of the real righteousness. Real righteousness is only related to duty. In the context of judiciary, righteousness and duty-bound karma are synonyms to each other. If a judge deviates from his duty-bound karma and delivers injustice instead of justice, it would be called Adharma or misdeed. This can also be called a crime. Every misdeed is actually a crime. Any misdeed i.e. a karma that harms justice and common good can never be Dharma. If Dharma does not have an aroma of justice, that it does not have the capacity to make a person righteous in real terms. Even a faint smell of injustice makes Dharma blemished. Thus there are two responsibilities for judiciary. Firstly, it should fulfill its duties i.e. deliver justice to the nation and

The demoniac elements or the criminal elements present in a society are the biggest hurdles in the path of duty-bound karma. Judiciary has the main responsibility for control ling those elements and destroying them.

all living beings without any discrimination, attachment, emotion and hatred, and secondly, it should enforce control on power and society so that the roots of injustice do not get stronger anywhere. Keeping a government under control is the right that judiciary has got from democracy. The main aim of the great phrase 'धर्मो रक्षति रक्षित:' ('*Dharmo Rakshati Rakshitah*') is to keep inspiring to follow the path of justice, and that is the reason this has been inscribed in golden letters above the seat of Chief Justice of the Supreme Court. This great phrase inscribed above the seat of Chief Justice is not meant only for the Supreme Court. The intention is that all seated officers, delivering justice across the country must protect Dharma i.e. duty-bound karma and justice, anyhow. They must also keep watch on the misdeeds of power and control it.

> *Indian philosophy has never presented Dharma in a narrow-minded or perverse form. Dharma is supreme, liberal and colossal. The purview of Dharma covers neither discrimination nor injustice nor favouritism nor emotion not hatred.*

Indian philosophy has never presented Dharma in a narrow-minded or perverse form. Dharma is supreme, liberal and colossal. The purview of Dharma covers neither discrimination nor injustice nor favouritism nor emotion not hatred nor affection nor attachment. It is nowhere connected to communalism and that is the reason that Dharma can be linked neither to any of the systems of worship nor to any specific religious scripture. Where there is welfare implied for all creatures, there is Dharma. Justice should be available not only to human beings but also to birds and animals, flora and fauna, rivers, springs, mountains and caves and the whole environment should be filled with Dharma. This is the spirit of 'धर्मो रक्षति रक्षित:' ('*Dharmo Rakshati Rakshitah*'). To safeguard this spirit is the supreme responsibility of justice. Let there be no stench of injustice anywhere - that is the advice to the judiciary. Indian philosophy believes that if the committee or any other such arrangement created for delivery of justice allows Dharma to get blemished and the judge does not energetically remove the unrighteous thorns in its path, they would destroy the whole system. This sentiment has been expressed in another shloka of Manusmriti in a very beautiful way. The shloka just before which contains the phrase 'धर्मो रक्षति रक्षितः' ('*Dharmo Rakshati Rakshitah*'), clearly mentions so. 'If Dharma is destroyed by Adharma and truth is scarred by untruth in an assembly, with members as onlookers, all those supporting that wrongdoing would ultimately get destroyed.'

"यत्र धर्मो हाधर्मेण सत्यं यत्रानृतेज चे।
हन्यते प्रेक्षमाणानां हतास्तत्र सभासदः ।।"

Just after the above shloka,
the following is written.
"धर्म एव हतो हंति धर्मो रक्षति रक्षितः।"

Humans not only should not exploit humans but they should also not exploit even environment, vegetation,water sources, mountains,flora and fauna.

In fact, this is the prime responsibility of a government to develop such a judiciary for common good, where a judge is able to protect truth without fear and put an end to injustice and exploitation. Indian philosophy is even not in favour of exploitation of Nature. Humans not only should not exploit humans but they should also not exploit even environment, vegetation, water sources, mountains, flora and fauna. Whatever is there in Nature has the right to get justice, and that also justice at all levels. In the eyes of justice, anybody is neither high nor low, big nor small, poor nor rich, king nor pauper. Justice should be devoid of emotion, hatred and discrimination. If, at the time of delivering justice, immediate requirements are given more importance than best values i.e. spirit of common good established by Dharma, that would be injustice. The way humans have today exploited Nature to solve their immediate problems and the way they have ignored the environment, the entire world is paying the price for it. The problem of the restoration of the environment that is being faced today has been created because governments did not create such class or system that would have ensured justice for each component of Nature. That is the reason why the future of human life appears to be difficult. When society or government strengthens injustice overtly or covertly, it definitely gives rise to exploitation. Hence, the sole responsibility of the judiciary is to ensure eradication of exploitation at all levels.

Indian philosophy has treated exploitation as a mental instinct. It does not make difference which class of society the exploiter comes from. Even the poorest of the poor may be an exploiter and the richest of the rich may belong to the category of exploiters. The point is that the tendency of exploitation may arise in a person or organisation at any level. Exploitation is such a mental disorder that may affect any section of society or any person any time. Exploitation is another form of injustice. Actually, it is an extremely perverted form of injustice. This instinct is the biggest hurdle in the path of common good. When a person or any organisation or section of society knowingly or unknowingly takes recourse to exploitation for satisfying his/its self-interest and ego, and judiciary tolerates it, that instinct takes the shape of character. When exploitation becomes a character of a person or society or class or organisation, various kinds of problems start appearing for humanity. Exploitation inflicted unknowingly or exploitation caused with an unintentional feeling may be pardoned for once, but the exploitation inflicted knowingly cannot be excused.

> *Indian philosophy has treated exploitation as a mental instinct. It does not make difference which class of society the exploiter comes from. Even the poorest of the poor may be an exploiter.*

Exploitation is an ideology that takes shape now and then and then disappears. It disappears because society does not accept it. Those who support the ideology of exploitation believe that exploitation cannot at all be removed from the existence of Mother Nature. When anything ends, something else is born and destruction is concealed in every creation. These are the kinds of arguments put forward in an attempt to get exploitation recognised. Humans have also faced such ideologies where exploitation was accepted as lifestyle and humans treated other humans worse than animals. However, there is no place for that kind of exploitation-oriented consciousness in the era we currently live with the development that human civilisation has attained. And with the way the whole world has accepted today the need for recognising human rights. Not only a human being would have to have a feeling of equality and magnanimity for other human beings, this feeling of magnanimity should be there for all creatures, for the entire Nature. The way the environment is getting unbalanced everywhere in today's world and the talks that are going on for making the environment pollution-free are also required to be seen in this context. This is the reason that the responsibility of judiciary has gone up tremendously today. In this context, there is a problem also as to how to protect the honour of justice. Today, new challenges keep cropping up even in front of justice at all levels. These challenges can be confronted only by accepting justice. Justice confronting challenges simply means that Dharma should stand in front of those challenges. Here, it is appropriate to repeat that justice and Dharma are just synonyms to each other. It would be ok only when justice itself safeguards its sovereignty, honour and existence. If justice is not able to protect its honour and sovereignty, politics would overwhelm justice. Millions of examples can be produced to show how attempts are being made to corrupt and pollute the judiciary today. Communism runs its entire politics only by recognising the principle of a committed justice. Indian people would have to be always vigilant to ensure that the idea of a committed judiciary is never developed in future. It would be the biggest danger for democracy if judiciary is taken over by politics. A situation of committed judiciary would be a big hurdle for human civilisation and development. This situation may be prevented - provided the judiciary remains vigilant. This vigilance of the judiciary should be constant and strict with no scope for delinquency at all. Even a minor lapse on the part of judiciary may allow political self-interest and ego to gain control over

The way the environment is getting unbalanced everywhere in today's world and the talks that are going on for making the environment pol lution-free are also required to be seen in this context.

it. Even if that situation does not come, it may still be possible that those who are responsible for delivering justice may get perverted by their own self-interest and self-ego. This has already happened in India. Here this cannot be forgotten how once politics had played with the Indian constitution and emergency was imposed on the country. The attitude of the Indian judiciary at that time was not worth admiring. The Indian judiciary at that time could protect its own sovereignty, its honour and its constitutional principles. Thus, the duty of justice is not only to prevent exploitation of society but also to prevent its own exploitation. Justice has even one more duty - it should not start exploiting itself. A situation of grave contradiction would arise if justice itself starts exploiting justice. There have been instances in many democratic countries when justice itself has exploited justice i.e. judiciary got perverted towards itself.

The attitude of the Indian judiciary at that time was not worth admiring. The Indian judiciary at that time could protect its own sovereignty, its honour and its constitutional principles.

If mysteries of duty-bound karma are to be uncovered, different levels of exploitation also need to be understood. There may be many levels of exploitation. As example, while humans do exploit humans on physical level, this exploitation may happen at mental and intellectual levels also. A person exploited at a physical level may of course be rescued. However, where exploitation is taking place at mental and intellectual levels, soon the situation comes to a shape such that the person being exploited is not even aware that he is being exploited and who is exploiting him. The exploitation inflicted at mental and intellectual levels ultimately gives rise to such hypnotism that the person does not even realise his suffering and plight. He loses all his capacity to resist. Innumerable examples are available to show the kind of hysteria humanity is suffering from because of intellectual exploitation. As an aftermath of intellectual exploitation, the person not only changes the philosophy and thinking of his life, he remains a subject of exploitation for those people for whom he is always ready to even risk his life. In the history of human civilisation, mental and intellectual exploitation that the society has undergone because of priestism and rituals have been creating situations of hysteria time and again. Rise in bigotry in our society is a result of the same mental and intellectual exploitation. This intellectual exploitation is the biggest hurdle in the path of healthy development and awakening of humanity. Today, the world is afflicted by this very exploitation at the most.

There are many kinds of intellectual exploitation. This is seen not only in spiritual domain but also in political, social, cultural and educational domains. The success that communism has achieved in politics is the result of intellectual exploitation. The recognition that dictatorship and royalism are receiving in different parts of the world today is the result of that state of hypnosis that was created by intellectual exploitation. The same intellectual and mental exploitation is also the fundamental reason for the feeling against colonialism existing in developed countries. The way this world is today afflicted by economic colonialism and modern colonialism, it cannot be cured until this maze of hypnotism is completely destroyed. When one nation attempts to impose its lifestyle and culture on another nation, that attempt should be definitely treated as a part of exploitation only. Some nations have assumed that they only are responsible for making the entire world civilised and they can impose their culture, ideology and lifestyle on every person on earth. This is gross injustice and is the most heinous example of cultural colonialism. Cultural colonialism is a form of exploitation only. If this exploitation is not stopped, this ever-expanding cultural colonialism may create many kinds of new problems in this world. The way wealthy countries of the West are always looking for opportunities to hypnotise people with their affluence and propaganda powers and the kinds of half-truths that are being used to encourage this process of hypnotism, are just creating new hurdles for development of mankind.

The way wealthy countries of the West are always looking for opportunities to hypnotise people with their affluence and propaganda powers and the kinds of half-truths that are being used to encourage this process.

Mankind would have to one day or other fight against the

materialistic and sensualistic culture adopted by wealthy countries of the West that are currently highly influenced by Christian missionaries. The sensualistic culture is itself sowing the seeds of its own destruction. What is expected is that a judiciary should be established at international level to resist this injustice and whatever platforms are available on international level to administer justice should be utilised. But how to create such an atmosphere? India may not be able to do much but at least it can give a clarion call for a war against this cultural colonialism and modern economic colonialism. To raise voice against injustice is duty-bound karma. It's the biggest weakness of mankind to tolerate injustice. Observing the way Anglo-centric consciousness is increasing its supremacy over Indian consciousness these days, Indian people probably may not be able to offer anything to the world in this respect.

Today,Indians have faith neither in their culture, history,philosophy nor in their values. An average Indian remains almost silent when Indian culture is criticised and dishonoured in front of him.

Today, Indians have faith neither in their culture, history, philosophy nor in their values. An average Indian remains almost silent when Indian culture is criticised and dishonoured in front of him. This is a serious problem in itself. How to awaken each and every Indian for resisting this expanding cultural colonialism? How to make him realise that he is being exploited both mentally and intellectually. It's not easy to find answers. This would be possible only when we Indians completely overhaul our education system. The consciousness that is required to make every Indian well-educated can be attained only by means of Indian languages. What about the current plight of Indian languages, who would rectify it and how? The circumstances currently are entirely opposite to the Indian consciousness. It's going to be extremely arduous to safeguard Indian consciousness and Indian culture in these hostile circumstances, as sensualistic system provides instant happiness and gratification. The glitter and glamour from the West has badly hypnotised an average Indian mind. This hypnosis is the reason for sense-centric sensualistic culture penetrating fast into Indian public life. This sensualistic culture today may also be called consumerism. Movements are being started in the name of safeguarding the rights of consumers. This also is a conspiracy. This conspiracy can be exposed only if Indian people are made aware of the problems being created by the evils of sensualistic culture and cultural colonialism coming from the West. Not only education but also all other publicity channels should be utilised to disseminate the awareness across the entire nation to educate the public about how the consumer-centric and sensualistic culture robs people of their virtues and how their lives become filled with struggles. Indian people must be made aware as to how this sensualistic culture creates unrest in their entire lives. Until that happens, it looks impossible to defeat the current cultural colonialism coming from the West. The question here is whether the Indian judiciary would be able to do anything against this cultural colonialism. Incidentally, this is the duty-bound karma of the Indian judiciary to express their thoughts against this storm coming from the West. In the context of duty-bound karma, this is very clear that 'duty-bound karma' gives rise to finest resolutions in a person and justice becomes impartial with the finest resolutions; there is no dispute in this. Where there is impartiality and equality, there is Dharma. But impartiality and equality does not mean that we remain silent and do not offer resistance against the cultures or classes or consciousness that are digging our roots and are ready to destroy us completely. Impartiality also does not mean that a person should bow his head and offer no resistance against a sinister aggressor. Such an interpretation of impartiality is chicanery. Impartiality means that neither we ourselves do injustice to anybody nor do we tolerate it being done to ourselves or anybody else. The person cannot be called impartial in real terms if he tolerates any injustice being meted out to him or injustice at any other levels. Dharma cannot be conceived in the absence of impartiality. Impartiality is also required to be understood properly. It would be gross ignorance to present the

This also is a conspiracy. This conspiracy can be exposed only if Indian people are made aware of the problems being created by the evils of sensualistic culture and cultural colonialism coming from the West.

philosophy of impartiality as chicanery. Resistance to *tamas* and attempt to eradicate untruth do not harm the philosophy of impartiality.

Impartiality has multiple forms. It has both an extrovert as well as an introvert form. In its extrovert form, this means recognising infinite varieties and showing amiable disposition towards all the varieties available in Nature. Any attempt to destroy the diversity is against the principles of impartiality. And hence, it becomes Dharma to oppose anybody who tries to destroy this diversity. In the external world, no two persons or creatures can ever have the same behaviour or same qualities. Every particle in Nature has its own uniqueness. How to safeguard whatever privacy and speciality each of the particles in Nature possesses is hidden in the philosophy of impartiality. This can be made possible only when a feeling of impartiality towards all is developed within our inner-selves. This spirit of impartiality within inner-self is the biggest achievement of philosophy. This awareness of the inner-self that only one consciousness is prevalent everywhere, only one divinity exists universally, which is one and whole, can make a human impartial in real terms.

Impartiality has multiple forms. It has both an extrovert as well as an introvert form. In its extrovert form, this means recognising infinite varieties and showing amiable disposition towards all the varieties available.

Impartiality does not mean that a bandit and a saint should be treated the same way or a criminal should not be punished. Removal of injustice is the main aim of impartiality. Injustice is a representation of Adharma. It is the prime responsibility of a judge, or anybody responsible for delivering justice, to refrain from injustice. Only when a judge has this awareness of his duty, he would be able to deliver justice impartially. It is required to be kept in mind that when a judge sits on the seat of justice, he cannot be assumed to be sitting in meditation. A judge sits in the state of dualism of this world. It becomes his duty to differentiate and judge on the basis of merits and demerits of Dharma and Adharma, justice and injustice and all the diversities on earth. But while forming an opinion in this context, his inner-self should be devoid of any jealousy, any feeling of dualism, any attachment and any ego. It is very clear that justice should be free from self-interest, ego, jealousy and hatred. At the level of this world, punishment as well as award has an existence. A judge would certainly have to be impartial in his inner-self while awarding a sentence or deciding on an award. Thus, being impartial also means that the inner-self has to be made completely free from self-interest, ego and jealousy. Only then Dharma would be protected, justice would be delivered and humanity would move towards its development.

□

8

Dharma and Science

The extroverted consciousness in which today's scientist resides, has made him not only too materialistic but too logical also. That which is being recognised as 'scientific intelligence' today, is actually stricken by a special kind of ego. The truth is that 'extremely logical intelligence' which cannot be called 'scientific intelligence'; but why would those egocentric scientists accept this? A scientist uses this 'extreme logic' only while interpreting the word Dharma. However, it is significant to note that whereas science does believe in the existence of logic, it does not recognise 'extreme logic'. Scientists believe that whatever they know is the only truth, and discovery of truth means disclosure of natural mysteries. It is assumed that mankind has been struggling with these mysteries since primitive days and has uncovered his mysteries by virtue of his intelligence and has also made Nature his partner in physical, mental and intellectual development. As today's extremely logical scientist does not believe in spiritual consciousness, he does not recognise the very existence of spiritual mystery. He treats any search for spiritual mysteries as only a misuse of time and intelligence. Modern science has been proclaiming this time and again that it does not have any interest in spirituality, as spiritualism is either chicanery or hypocrisy or superstition. A scientific mind busy in a laboratory has no interest in either 'paramatma' or 'Dharma'; this is the reason that the scientific mind does not consider 'Dharma' of any use to science.

Scientific minds of the West have understood 'Dharma' only as self-serving rituals, prayers and worships, hypocritical pronouncements and a vision accepting the concepts of heaven and hell. These imaginations of heaven and hell linked to Dharma have been born out of the concept of power to give awards and punishments. Western mind does not interpret Dharma the way it has been interpreted in Indian Upanishads and Vedanta philosophy. The Vedanta philosophy and the principles and values articulated it do not match with those of any of the Western thinkers who treat themselves as religious thinkers. The fact is that establishment of Vedanta in the form of Dharma does not get impacted at all by the concepts of heaven and hell or individualistic divine existence. In the West, Dharma just means principles, commandments, directives and pronouncements contained in a book and instructions and rituals received from some 'extremely conscious existence'. Indian philosophers, and especially the Vedantists, refute this understanding completely. Vedanta philosophy believes that there is no such power or existence that resides in some special world. Who provides directions and instructions to mankind, makes pronouncements and decides on sending a pious person to heaven and sinners to hell.

The Vedanta philosophy and the principles and values articulated it do not match with those of any of the Western thinkers who treat themselves as religious thinkers. The fact is that establishment of Vedanta in the form of Dharma.

The perversity of Western scientists in the context of Dharma has entered India also. The mind of Indian scientists has also started to see 'Dharma' through Western glasses. Speaking of Upanishad-based consciousness, an Indian scientist's mind either is indifferent or ignores it or remains silent or is stricken with perversity. It is the same as the one that has taken over atheistic and Christianity-centric scientific mind of the West. However, the eternal form of 'Dharma' and its interpretations supported by the Upanishads cannot be destroyed by any atheist. It cannot be harmed also by the concepts and pronouncements based on self-serving and narrow-minded consciousness and developed in Arab, Mesopotamia, Syria or Philistine. The ideology that was developed by Semitic countries for internal development of a person, removal of his misery and leading him to joy and prosperity, was coined as 'Dharma' by the West. For the West, these very pronouncements, systems and directions and instructions for regulating life are Dharma. Western philosophers and scientists use this very Semitic ideology as the base for evaluation, estimation and analysis of spiritual thinking of the entire world. Unfortunately, the Indian mind, influenced by Western culture, civilisation and lifestyle, is also accepting or adopting it slowly. It does not want to even have a look towards the robust knowledge of Upanishads.

The scientific mind of the West does accept the existence of morality but does not accept the existence of righteousness. Science believes that it is not necessary to be righteous to be moral. Even an atheist can be moral. Accordingly, the greatest morality is possibly found in this age only in those people who do not believe in existence of God. And abominable morality is found mostly in countries like India, which has the largest number of saints and hermits and has some or other God or Goddess seated at every crossing. But, of the two - theist and atheist, who is superior? Answer to this is not as easy as has been assumed by the West. In order to understand Dharma, the West would have to, first of all, get rid of all those prejudices that they have nurtured in respect of 'Dharma'. The interpretation that the West has provided for 'Dharma' does not match at all with the interpretation presented by Indian philosophy.

The scientific mind of the West does accept the existence of morality but does not accept the existence of righteousness. Science believes that it is not necessary to be righteous to be moral. Even an atheist can be moral.

Righteousness makes a person theist, as being righteous is in itself an internal transformation. This is a unique transformation. Only after this internal transformation do all the behaviours of a person start working under the influence of consciousness of non-duality. He who is truly righteous goes beyond both morality and immorality. The behaviour of a righteous person is not induced only by morality; rather it goes much ahead. Germination of righteous consciousness takes place from oneness-centred consciousness. That is the reason why behaviours of those who are really righteous, are extremely mysterious. The concept of good and bad is linked to the beliefs of society; though, righteous saints like Kabir, Buddha, Mahavira, Muhammad and Jesus knowingly violated many of the beliefs of society and provided the society fresh revolutionary values. The behaviour of Mahavira or dealings of Jesus cannot be constrained by common limits of morality.

'Dharma' is the process of understanding the Supreme Oneness of this creation. The personality of a true righteous person gets transformed completely after understanding Supreme Oneness. 'There is only one Param Chaitanya' - this feeling of inner-self is possible only by means of Dharma. Yes, after the latest researches that science has made, it is becoming apparent that science and Dharma, both are reaching the same place. Science, while analysing the matter, has concluded that the entire world is an extension or network of electric energy. Science also believes that this all-pervading electric energy has neither a beginning nor an end. This energy is permanent, everlasting and eternal. The same energy that science knows as electricity is referred to as 'Param Chaitanya' by 'Dharma' or spirituality. Dharma claims that everything is a form of Param Chaitanya only. This very Param Chaitanya is *Paramatma*. Both Dharma and science appear to be agreeing on this point that whatever comes in contact with us is actually the extension of 'One'. However, the way a righteous person transforms his mind to reach and understand this 'One', science does not change his mind to discover 'electric energy' and hence it remains untouched by 'Param Chaitanya'. As the mind of a scientist does not change, his self is not transformed at all, whereas Dharma transforms the inner-self and proclaims 'You change your mind, your behaviour would change on its own'.

This very Param Chaitanya is Paramatma. Both Dharma and science appear to be agreeing on this point that whatever comes in contact with us is actually the extension of 'One'.

Until sometime back, science believed that fundamentally there were two elements in this creation - one of the elements was matter and the other was electric energy. However, science has now arrived at the final conclusion in this regard. After fissions of molecules and atoms, it has found that everything is just an electric energy. Today's science accepts that the thing that we treat as matter is also actually an extremely condensed form of electric energy. Science, however is not able to clarify why this electric energy appears as a solid object on extreme condensation. Here comes the difference in perceptions of Dharma and science. Dharma maintains that there is nothing like solid or liquid, and whatever appears as solid is although looking like solid is actually not solid. Science maintains that whatever is solid is actually solid only. This mystery of Dharma can be understood by science only when it becomes ready to transform its inner-self. Nobody knows when this is going to happen. However, in short, the conclusion that science has arrived at in respect of electric energy is exactly the same as the conclusion arrived at by Dharma in respect of spirituality. It is Dharma of the energy of Chaitanya to contain an entire creation. As per spirituality, Chaitanya is the basis for entire creation. This Chaitanya can be understood as life energy also and it is eternal, true, endless and infinite. But the electric energy that is flowing in molecules and atoms can be treated as Param Chaitanya as per spiritual consciousness. That energy is definitely flowing under some or other arrangement. The system under which this electric energy is flowing in molecules and atoms is actually the Dharma of molecules and atoms. Any object that is created by combination of molecules and atoms is also constrained by some or other set of regulations. This set of regulations and discipline among these molecules and atoms is their Dharma in spiritual language. If a molecule of a matter renounces its Dharma and starts behaving in a chaotic manner, the existence of that matter would cease immediately.

Dharma maintains that there is nothing like solid or liquid,and whatever appears as solid is although looking like solid is actual ly not solid. Science maintains that whatever is solid is actual ly solid only.

The main foundations of science are logic and experiment. Experiment has to be such that it could be performed by anybody using his intelligence and specific instruments. Science goes up to the extreme end of logic to perform an experiment and tries to understand all those aspects of extrovert life that get impacted by the experiment. In a sense, science may be treated as the discoverer of mysteries; but Dharma is, in a sense, such a mystery that can be understood only by being introvert. Extrovert consciousness cannot even uncover the mysteries of Dharma or perform any experiment for it.

Science talks of fission of matter for its experiments and Dharma talks of synthesis, connection and union. If an object is given to science for experiment, it would first of all break the object into pieces whereas Dharma is against fragmentation at any level. Dharma, instead, talks of oneness and totality. Dharma has found, after introverted consciousness, cogitation and experiments, that the fundamental power is that of the whole and not of a fragment. This whole only appears as a fragment but this appearance is only a misperception. This totality and entirety has been given the name of 'Param Chaitanya'. That Param Chaitanya only is *Parameshwara*, the Supreme Being.

Science talks of fission of matter for its experiments and Dharma talks of synthesis, connection and union. If an object is given to science for experiment, it would first of all break the object into pieces.

Parameshwara is not a consciousness in physical state or living state. Parameshwara or Paramatma is an experience, an introverted realisation. Paramatma is also not a principle and not a philosophy that could be attained by arguments or debates. Paramatma also is not available in books, religious scriptures, interpretations or discourses. When a person wants to fall in love, he would have to first become a lover himself; then only he can experience love. Similarly, if anybody wants to know Paramatma, he would have to become paramatma himself i.e. he would have to completely renounce his egocentric body and mind and intellect-centric existence; he would have to get immersed in the feeling of paramatma. Paramatma cannot be attained without getting fully immersed in the consciousness of Paramatma.

Those who want to find Paramatma through the path of doctrines, those who wish to understand Dharma through the path of principles, are actually straying. Those who want to understand Paramatma or Dharma only through their intelligence are also going astray, as intelligence is just an instrument. The instrument of intelligence is certainly required to understand the *whole* but only to a limited extent. To enter the state of totality, this instrument of intelligence would have to be ultimately abandoned and then only real faith and devotion would emerge there. Faith and devotion only helps a person find that door which he may use to enter the state of bliss. Life is a colossal power and the brain is only a very small component of it. Intelligence is an extremely minute form of that colossal energy. This intelligence is dependent on our senses only. If the number of senses are increased, our experience also would change. Hence, only when we renounce the feeling of senses and also renounce the feeling of mind and intelligence, we may gain entry, slowly, to the supreme consciousness of the inner-self that is required to understand the colossal power of life. This is a mystery for science. Definitely, God is a supreme mystery and that would remain a supreme mystery only, as nobody knows where from this Param Chaitanya that is called electric energy by science, has come. Science wants to perform experiments on the life force, Chaitanya. However, that is not possible, as he who has to perform the experiment is himself a minute form of Param Chaitanya only. Experiment on the *whole* by a fragment is impossible.

> *The instrument of intel ligence is certainly required to understand the whole but only to a limited extent. To enter the state oftotality,this instrument ofintel ligence would have to be ultimately abandoned.*

The West is conducting research on introvert life, but it has not been able to reach anywhere till now, as all the researches are being conducted with dualism-centred i.e. self-serving consciousness only. This dualism-centred consciousness is always attained by domination of extrovert existence. Western philosophers could not understand whether there is any definite place for supreme oneness even in the consciousness of duality. The consciousness of non-duality is based on spirituality. Spirituality means study, contemplation, cogitation and analysis of the existence of self. The West has recognised the human personality only on three levels - physical, mental and intellectual. Apart from these three levels, science does accept existence of the element of 'life' but also maintains that the purpose of the element of life is to keep body, mind and intelligence together. Indian philosophy or spiritualism mentions one more level other than above four levels, that is - 'spiritual level'. Attainment of bliss is possible only after going into this spiritual level. Modern scientists refuse to accept this analysis, terming it as hypocrisy or superstition. This ignorance of modern science today with regard to spiritual consciousness is regrettable as well as worrying. In a sense, this is the perversity of modern science. This very level of spiritual consciousness provides the personality maximum power and completeness; but that level can be attained only when the most intense curiosity arises in the inner-self. Of course, it cannot be said that this curiosity did not arise in the West; the curiosity did awaken, but not fully. This can be said so because, despite attaining all the material prosperity, peace and happiness, the West is getting pulled apart all around. The scientist's mind is not able to experience a life filled with eternal peace despite all its efforts. According to Indian philosophers, "The fundamental character of mankind is transcendental truth and this character is covered with multiple layers of different shells." These layers are called *'Kosha'* in Vedanta. There are five koshas. The first of them is the biggest kosha.

Indian philosophy or spiritualism mentions one more level other than above four levels, that is - 'spiritual level'. Attainment of bliss is possible only after going into this spiritual level. Modern scientists refuse to accept this analysis.

This is 'Annamaya Kosha' that forms the existence of body i.e. the existence of physical self. Chaitanya in its inanimate form resides in this 'Annamaya Kosha' only. Next is 'Pranamaya Kosha' and then still minuter is 'Manomaya Kosha'. The next kosha that is still more minute compared to Manomaya Kosha is called 'Vigyanmaya Kosha'. A person gets his intellectual power from this Vigyanmaya Kosha. The mind keeps on making resolutions and choices, whereas intelligence provides finality to those resolutions and choices. Intelligence is finer than the mind. The kosha that is still finer than 'Vigyanmaya Kosha' is called 'Anandamaya Kosha' in Vedanta. The feeling under Anandamaya Kosha is almost same as the feeling of idleness or peace in sleep. Whatever be the condition of a person, whatever be his status in society, when he is in deep slumber he experiences the same common kind of peace. After entering this kosha, known matters are not experienced, rather only pleasure is experienced. This realisation of a delightful experience of deep slumber should be available perpetually in the worldly life - this is the endeavour of Dharma. This realisation can be attained only when we understand the true nature of our soul i.e. the supreme spirit. Knowledge of true nature of the supreme spirit would only help uncover the mysteries of Dharma. Western science neither understands the mysteries of the supreme spirit nor the mysteries of Anandamaya Kosha.

That which is called 'Dharma' by India is not individualistic and self-serving like 'Dharma' or 'religion' of the West. Vedanta does not call any cult or system of prayers and worship as Dharma. Vedanta knows Dharma only in its best form having liberalness and the feeling of common good. In this form, Dharma also is a science. In its highly liberal and common good-oriented form, Dharma becomes an eternal element and provides a mode for attaining peace, happiness and balance. The non-communal and common good-oriented character of Dharma is not constrained either by interpretation by any specific person or by any specific scripture. This common good-oriented Dharma completely rejects the existence of separation while believing fully in the existence of supreme oneness, and desires welfare for all. Dharma clearly defines the path for awakening the feelings of love, brotherhood, cordiality and oneness and removal of depravity from inner-self. The aim of Dharma is to awaken oneness-centred consciousness, that is common good-oriented and free from discrimination. And to treat the entire earth as its own form and to behave with the feeling of brotherhood. Dharma, in this character, is a successful science for growth in life.

That which is called 'Dharma' by India is not individualistic and self-serving like 'Dharma' or 'religion' of the West. Vedanta does not call any cult or system of prayers and worship as Dharma.

A restless and unbalanced mind can provide neither prosperity nor happiness nor pleasure. 'Dharma' is the science for making the mind peaceful, stable, creative and happy. Mind can move towards supreme peace and happiness only if the person knows the art of looking into his inner-self. Only by looking into inner-self can a person recognise the real eternal character of self. The main objection of scientists in recognising Dharma as science is that it nourishes traditionalism and conventionalism. However, this objection is not correct. The truth is that modern science itself requires a conventional course for its development; no such thing is required for righteousness. All those discoveries and inventions that mankind has achieved during the last thousands of years have only been used as the foundations by the modern science for its development. Just for example, bullock carts would not have been made if wheels were not invented, inventions of bicycle and car would have been impossible without the development of bullock carts. And it was the construction of the bicycle that gave the clues to the Wright Brothers for development of airplanes. The Indian concept of 'Dharma' is neither traditional not conventional. Whereas, science cannot stand in front of it even for a moment if it relinquishes all those inventions and discoveries that have been achieved in the world of science in the last hundreds of years.

> *A restless and unbalanced mind can provide neither prosperity nor happiness nor pleasure. 'Dharma' is the science for making the mind peaceful,stable, creative and happy. Mind can move towards supreme peace.*

Though there are many arguments and interpretations available in the context of Dharma and science, the kind of excellent interpretation and thoughts that Shri Rajneesh has provided is rarely seen anywhere else. Rajneesh has established Dharma in the form of a science and he refers to it as knowledge. In the 11th chapter of his book, '*Main Mrityu Sikhata Hun*', Rajneesh states that 'Science does not mean that we have conquered nature. There is no way to conquer nature. Science only means that we have discovered some methods to live according to nature. There is no other meaning for science. Can we really conquer? And who would conquer whom? We have found ways to live according to nature.

"Nature was ready to run a fan for a long time. We were just not able to fix the fan at the right place. Did you understand me? The wind outside was always ready to blow, but we had constructed the walls. We did not provide any window. When we construct a window, would you claim that we have conquered wind? We have only left the passages for the wind open. Wind is always ready to blow. If we are running fans on electricity and putting on the lights, we have not conquered nature anyway. We have just found the way to be compatible to nature. Now we fix our bulbs with that compatibility, fix our switches with that compatibility and spread our wires with that compatibility so that electricity may pass through the same. It was always ready to pass through. We are just opening the window.

"Science is the discovery of the compatibilities with nature - external nature. And Dharma is discovery of the compatibilities of the internal rules of nature. There are rules of nature in the external world and nature becomes cooperative if we go according to them and it becomes uncooperative if we go against them. In a sense, it is not correct to say that nature is cooperative or uncooperative. Instead, it would be appropriate to say whether we are able to get cooperation from nature or not. Thus, we should say that if we stand in a way that nature is able to be cooperative, we take advantage of nature. If we stand in a way that nature is not able to be cooperative, we suffer harm.

Science is the discovery of the compatibilities with nature - external nature. And Dharma is discovery of the compatibilities of the internal rules of nature. There are rules of nature in the external world and nature becomes cooperative.

"If you are walking with an umbrella and the wind is blowing towards you and you tilt your umbrella in front of you, it would be ok. If you keep the umbrella on the back side on your shoulder, the wind would throw it back. There is no fault of nature in this. You just did not keep the umbrella in a compatible manner. Just that, is your responsibility. Nature is working the same way in both the cases. When you keep the umbrella in front of you, it is still pressing the umbrella, but pressing towards you. When you keep the umbrella on your shoulder, it is pressing then also, but it is pressing away from you. It is just the way you hold the umbrella.

"Similarly, there are internal rules of nature also. A person who is living the life with anger, he is keeping the umbrella on his shoulder. Now he would certainly get into troubles. All his internal umbrellas would be destroyed. And the person who is spreading love, he is keeping his umbrella in front of him. He is getting compatible with nature. Thus, the person who knows how to love has actually learnt one of the rules of internal science. He has learnt that love brings compatibility to the internal life and anger only generates incompatibilities for the internal life. This also is just like the case of gravitation. Legs are broken under anger while love heals broken legs. Nature is ready to do its job in both the cases. It all depends on what you are doing. A person in anger is jumping from the roof.

"The last compatibility of the inner world is meditation. Last compatibility means deepest of the deep compatibility. Meditation means that the person is now standing internally compatible with the supreme rule of life. Hence, the name Tao that Lao Tse has given to it is acceptable. Tao means rule. Or, the name that the architects of Vedas have given is correct. That name is *'Rit'. Rit* means the law. Similarly, the meaning of Dharma is the same - rules. Dharma means character, the law. Dharma means the rules that you follow, such that, if you follow the same you would attain happiness. Adharma means doing things that are against the rules and then you would attain grief.

Dharma means character,the law. Dharma means the rules that you fol low,such that,if you fol low the same you would attain happiness. Adharma means doing things that are against the rules.

"This is a matter of internal science and meditation is the process of becoming compatible in a real sense, in the internal sense. We should call it compatibility if the person is compatible in all respects, if he does not fight with life anywhere and if he does not get separated from life any way. A person who has become compatible with all the rules of life in all respects attains supreme truth, supreme life, bliss and supreme salvation. And we are also standing below the same rules, but we keep fighting against the same rules and attain the supreme bondage. Fighting against the same rules! That means, the situation is something like this that some people who understand gold, get the same cast into ornaments while some others who cannot understand gold get the same cast into chains. The rule of the gold is the same. The rule of moulding is the same. The rule of casting is the same. Now it all depends on you whether you want to cast an ornament or a chain.

"He who is able to accomplish his internal compatibility completely with the rules of nature attains Dharma. He who accomplishes compatibility completely on the outer side attains science.

"What we get out of Dharma is called *'gyan'* i.e. knowledge. What we get out of science is called *'vigyan'* i.e. a branch of knowledge. Both these words are very meaningful. We are not attaching any prefix in gyan, not adding any adjective. Vigyan means special knowledge. And gyan means just simple knowledge, nothing special. Thus, Dharma means the understanding of getting easy with internal nature of life. Hence, that is just gyan - just knowing, not any specialised knowledge. Vigyan is a specialised knowledge. Vigyan is special knowledge, as in every area we have to find out - what would be the compatibility for this rule or that rule, and rules are in crores.

Vigyan is a specialised knowledge. This is the knowledge ofeach and every ray,hence it is specialised. If anybody concentrates on one ray ofvigyan,he would understand that ray only. The deeper he goes, the more knowledge he gains.

"Naturally, the more we go inside, the less would be the number of rules. The more we go outside, the more would be the number of rules. If we start drawing lines from a point in all directions, all lines going out would be one at the point but as they go out they would be spreading out. The farther they go from the point, the more would be the distance between two lines - just like the rays of sun spreading around. All the rays are one only at the sun, but as they move away from sun, the number of rays goes on increasing, they go on spreading and the distance between the rays goes on increasing.

"Vigyan is a specialised knowledge. This is the knowledge of each and every ray, hence it is specialised. If anybody concentrates on one ray of vigyan, he would understand that ray only. The deeper he goes, the more knowledge he would get for still finer rays; but then the ray would be getting finer and the more he goes farther, the more the ray would become fine. Vigyan, hence would go on getting finer and narrower. Dharma would continue to get larger, greater and more abstract. In the end, only non-duality would exist. There wouldn't be anything two there. That's why I say that there may be many vigyans but there cannot be many Dharmas. There can be only one Dharma as that is knowledge, not a specialised knowledge."

Science claims that it provides prosperity and authority, and mankind has attained all the material happiness because of science only. Definitely, this claim of science is correct in many respects. They have faulted in one respect only and that is that whatever great scientists and inventors of the world have achieved is all because of their mental balance, peace and will power only. This mental balance, peace and will power are attained by a person only after becoming an introvert and self-controlled. Dharma teaches us the approach as to why and how to get introverted and self-controlled. The disquiet and disarray in the inner-self is the biggest reason for a person's misery. There may be many reasons for disquiet, dissatisfaction, turmoil, disarray and restlessness. None of the material prosperity can bring peace to mind and also cannot remove the darkness of inner-self. Nobody has ever got satisfied with wealth, authority, power and enjoyment. Power, property, enjoyment and strength only provide hope, dream and misconception of happiness; but dreams are never fulfilled. Dharma is that science that provides peace and happiness for the inner-self; material prosperity can be attained, authority can be attained and even strength can be acquired by following Dharma.

If a merger of modern science and real Dharma is made possible, it may give rise to an innovative revolution. A new mankind may be born out of this merger. Dharma and science together are capable of building such a universe.

If a merger of modern science and real Dharma is made possible, it may give rise to an innovative revolution. A new mankind may be born out of this merger. Dharma and science together are capable of building such a universe that would be divine and that would be capable of providing spiritual completeness. Creation of a complete human being is possible only by a balanced blending of Dharma and modern science. A divine life is such an enduring experience where there is no place for mental disquiet and fear, bitterness and disputes, narrow-mindedness and exploitation. There is only consciousness of common good-oriented eternal existence, there is bliss.

A pure and pious mind, a mind brimming with peace and happiness ultimately provides fundamental completeness. This mind, that has become powerful and complete by means of Dharma, is no way a hindrance for science; rather it is supremely helpful for science. Knowledge of the inner-self only fills a person with real and permanent confidence. One thing that needs to be understood is that mind is a flow of thoughts and the quality of thoughts builds the internal and external personality. Hence, the art of attaining that quality and nourishing and augmenting the same would have to be learnt. There is a science even for enriching the ideological quality and removal of ignorance and that is what we call as 'Dharma'.

Dharma is a vast science. It is of great use to the world. We are not talking of Dharma that is related to rituals of ringing bells and performing aarti. We are referring to that Dharma that helps a person in the quest.

An absolute pundit and propagator of Gita knowledge, late Swami Chinmayanand has presented this in a very nice way in his book '*Atmavikas Ki Nirdeshika*'. According to him, "This has been said very emphatically by maharishis of ancient times that the knowledge of the internal spiritual structure of a person helps him in taking ownership of his life. Spiritual teachers analysed the personality of the person coming in contact with external world. They discovered those instruments and internal distinctions that helped a person get the experience of life. They regulated, refined and organised those instruments and found out how a person could attain maximum success and happiness in his life. This very mystery has been mentioned in all the sacred scriptures – be it a

Hindu, Muslim, Christian scripture or a Buddhist scripture or a scripture belonging to any other Dharma in this world.

"Dharma is a vast science. It is of great use to the world. We are not talking of Dharma that is related to rituals of ringing bells and performing aarti. We are referring to that Dharma that helps a person in the quest for his internal power so that he could stand up bravely to face the challenges of life. As also live his life serving other people sincerely with the help of the concepts obtained from science. In a real sense, that only which can help a person to live his life in the external world with honesty and confidence is Dharma. It is the science of re-evaluation of life. Just like scientists perform their research work in their laboratories, Indian saints used to visit serene and cool valleys of Himalayas for experiments on human life. The external world has been the subject of research for scientists, whereas the subject of experiments by the saints has been the inner-world of the experiences of humans. Scientists want to know 'What is this world?' and saints want to understand 'What is a human?'. "

Dharma cautions us not to indulge in unnecessary self-destructive efforts. We should learn to differentiate between important and trivial, permanent and temporary,full l and empty.

In the same book, Swami Chinmayananda has mentioned, "Materialism is very nice, there is no doubt in that; but that makes the worries and cravings infinite for a person. He starts to earn and accumulate more and more wealth and indulge in luxuries. The person becomes naturally thoughtless and wants to enjoy sensual pleasures. He toils for momentary satisfaction of physical passion, mental desire and intellectual hunger. Today, more people are dying due to worries than those because of labour - is this not a well-known fact? The person today just creates mental tension on trivial matters and wastes his valuable time for nothing. He treats it as civilisation; however, careful and cautious people understand that usefulness of our life lies only in taking our civilisation to completeness.

"Dharma cautions us not to indulge in unnecessary self-destructive efforts. We should learn to differentiate between important and trivial, permanent and temporary, full and empty. We should try our best to engage our valuable life in the attainment of permanency and completeness.

"We should stand straight and careful with the pride of our human life and move forward to attain the highest level of humanity i.e. our divine character."

If a person has to attain completeness in life and provide a new divine life to his fragmented and restive personality, he would have to be encouraged to stand with confidence. This is possible only by accepting the existence of Dharma, there is no other way for him. Whatever attempts modern science makes, it cannot provide real happiness and enjoyment to humanity. And this without, regulating the inner life, and taking support and assistance from Dharma.

□

9

Dharma and Communalism

To understand the essence of Dharma, it may be divided into two forms. One is the form that has been named as 'Param Dharma' by Indian philosophers after intensive introverted realisation. The other one is 'Conventional Dharma', that which is understood by a common person in his worldly life and is operated and influenced by rituals and priestism.

'Param Dharma' is neither a philosophy nor a set of rituals. This is such an eternal element that can be attained only by realisation; rather it may be enough to mention here that 'Param Dharma' is a realisation. The basis for this realisation is 'Supreme Consciousness' i.e. undivided uninterrupted and complete consciousness. On the other hand, 'Conventional Dharma' is born out of the ignorance of divided consciousness. This 'Conventional Dharma' is egocentric and based on self-interest. This is nourished and developed by the consciousness that believes in the existence of detachment and separation.

'Conventional Dharma' has many forms; hence it may have infinite concepts. Today, people have fabricated 'Conventional Dharma' in different ways for their own benefit and self-interest or to gain happiness and enjoyment. The kinds of Dharma as perceived by egocentric and self-serving consciousness have their own principles, concepts and necessities and their own separate priests. Moreover, even their concepts of life and death, heaven and hell do not match significantly with each other. This 'Conventional Dharma' is known in this world by different names like Hindu Dharma, Muslim Dharma, Christian Dharma and Buddha Dharma. In reality, they are not Dharmas, instead they are just sects or communities. However, these doctrines and heresies have come into practice so much that all these are referred to as Dharma. As of date, it is very difficult to demolish this conventional concept of Dharma, and demolishing it is also not going to provide any instant benefit. Any effort to demolish the same would mean invitation to enmities, war, bloodshed and unrest. Hence, people are compelled to remain in the ignorance of 'Conventional Dharma'. Self-interest and ego has got blended with this deformation and misconception of Dharma so much that a normal person has forgotten the real concepts of Dharma and started to believe in this much-divided consciousness as truth. Hence, efforts should be made to develop respect and feeling of equality among people and end the aggressiveness that exists between each other. Currently, development of the situation of 'all Dharmas are equal' and does not appear to be in sight. Most of the Dharmas that have come into existence out of divided and self-serving consciousness are flourishing only because of their ego, self-interest and aggressiveness. This very aggressiveness in the guise of Dharma is 'communalism'. This aggressiveness has been adopted somewhere due to political reasons, somewhere due to economic reasons and somewhere else due to social reasons. Today, the situation has become such that money power, deceit and muscle power are being used freely to impose their so-called religious philosophy on others. That also in the name of development of culture and civilisation. If it were only the issue of love, affection and belief towards one's own Dharma, communalism would not have been treated as such a demon. However, the issue does not remain limited to faith and belief in one's own Dharma, instead continuous attempts are being made to expand, by whatever means possible, one's own values and beliefs at any cost. This not only provides gratification for one's ego, but also facilitates political and financial gains. In a sense, this 'Dharma' i.e. 'Conventional Dharma' has become a tool for the exploitation of humanity.

Most of the Dharmas that have come into existence out of divided and self-serving consciousness are flourishing only because of their ego, self-interest and aggressiveness. This very aggressiveness in the guise of Dharma is 'communalism'.

Whatever be the reasons for communalism, their clear identification may be lot more easier if we look towards the philosophical side of divided consciousness. The first thing that needs to be understood is that consciousness is in reality uninterrupted and eternal; but appears divided and limited by time due to misconceptions. This divided consciousness has made mankind extremely restless in his inner-self. Whatever be the extent of talks of peace that this mankind indulges in and whatever be the extent of means of happiness and enjoyment that he accumulates, his mind remains restless. This mankind with a restless and agitated mind looks for peace in external instruments and hence his disorientation is increasing and his inner-self is getting constantly filled with contradictions. The restlessness of mankind devoid of social harmony and real peace is slowly moving towards derangement. This restlessness only pushes him towards hypocrisy, compels him to follow fanaticism and conservatism and even provides emphasis to communal virulence. The principle is that the more a person is restless, the more he would be perverse and in the language of religious domain, the more he would be communal.

The main aim of real Dharma is to go beyond the ignorance of divided consciousness and attain supreme peace and happiness. The goal of Dharma is the removal of misconceptions and ignorance arising from separation.

The main aim of real Dharma is to go beyond the ignorance of divided consciousness and attain supreme peace and happiness. The goal of Dharma is the removal of misconceptions and ignorance arising from separation. But the reality is that this removal also would have to be done through realisation at a personal level only. In this sense, the existence of the feeling of separation cannot be denied at a temporal level. Just as the existence of a wave in an ocean cannot be denied, separation as the wave in the ocean of Supreme Chaitanya will have to be accepted; but it has to be kept in mind that the real existence is that of the ocean and not of the wave. Now that there is existence of separation i.e. duality at the temporal level, the existence of a person also gets acceptance, and in that case, existence of ego of every person also will have to be accepted. The consciousness of existence is possible only because of ego; hence, if separation is to be eliminated, ego would have to be conquered. But this job is not easy, rather it is extremely difficult as this ego is by nature selfish, expansionist and aggressive. This nature of ego may be restrained by practice, but this cannot be eliminated until the existence of this world. Thus, this is to be understood that various Dharmas coming under 'Conventional Dharma' would definitely remain communal somehow or other - this is their helplessness. If these conventional Dharmas do not remain communal, their very existence would be lost. Conventional consciousness is extroverted consciousness. It is temporal consciousness and accepts the existence of separation and resides in it. Hence ego and self-interest are, in a sense, their life elements. It is clear that external consciousness-oriented conventional Dharmas cannot be reformed as non-communal and complete humanitarian. A consciousness that is anti-communal and has awareness of the welfare of all creatures would emerge only when ego and self-interest start to disappear. This is possible with the thinking of 'आत्मवत् सर्वभूतेषु' (*'Atmavat Sarvabhuteshu'* i.e. feel the happiness and distress of others as your own). Contemplation of 'आत्मवत् सर्वभूतेषु' is not an easy one; rather it is an introverted realisation that is attained by practice and elimination of ego. This common good-oriented contemplation cannot be attained through conventional Dharmas. This nonmaterial and ego-free colossal contemplation cannot be given any name. Still, in reference to contemplation, this may be addressed as 'Param Dharma' or 'Rit Dharma (ऋत धर्म)'. 'Param Dharma' does not have any connection with communalism.

This common good-oriented contemplation cannot be attained through conventional Dharmas. This nonmaterial and ego-free colossal contemplation cannot be given any name.

Communalism cannot be part of creation or the whole; its emergence itself is from the divided consciousness. Param Chaitanya starts appearing as divided with egocentric contemplation. As ego goes up, separation and division goes on growing in the same proportion. This separation-centric and divided existence struggles to protect its character and goes on getting more and more communal on the levels of behaviour and conduct.

Whenever consciousness resides in the separation of 'I' and 'You', and the more it resides there, it would grow more and more communal and divided. There is no way to save the consciousness that believes in 'I' and 'You' from communal appeals. Communalism is itself the natural product of divided consciousness. This fact can also be stated as something like this - communalism is the character of divided consciousness. The more the consciousness is divided in inner-self, the more it would be communal also. The man of today is directed by conventional consciousness and hence he resides in divided consciousness only. His entire conduct and his entire mental and intellectual milieu depend on this much-divided consciousness. Hence, in order to build up his self-interest, he looks for persons having similar thoughts and creates a group and organisation with them. Communalism, after reaching this group-oriented status, becomes capable of strengthening its roots still further. These deep roots of communalism only provide specific nourishment to separation and arrogance.

Arrogance and self-interest have a specific character that they are always zealous for their accretion. Arrogance wants its perpetual expansion, its sovereignty and only its recognition.

Arrogance and self-interest have a specific character that they are always zealous for their accretion. Arrogance wants its perpetual expansion, its sovereignty and only its recognition. Arrogance gets pleasure only when anybody sings its admiration; it wants respect and recognition in any situation. This expansionist and sensualist character of arrogance makes it more and more communalist. This is the reason that nobody can save 'Conventional Dharma', emerging from divided consciousness, from turning communalist. Those who think that conventional Dharma-centred consciousness may be persuaded against communalism. And this, by creating constitution or enacting strict laws and regulations or chanting slogans for treating all of them equal are making a mistake. Communalism can never be destroyed completely by constitution, laws or state orders. Even the strictest of laws or any other measure may at best have only partial control on communalism. The poison of communalism, on the other hand, quietly keeps its roots intact and whenever it gets even a slightly favourable environment, it blows out in the open. The main reason for the failures that humanity is facing in eliminating the poison of communalism is that the philosophy of communalism has not been understood properly. The remedies applied on the outer level may result in some instant and partial restraint, but they have been completely unsuccessful in the eradication of communalism.

Existence of tolerance and liberality along with communalism is impossible. Once communalism creates its space, it makes all possible efforts for its expansion. Communalism cannot be kept in control for long just on the strength of power and law. As this temperament is fully linked to arrogance and self-interest, it looks for new methods and ways for its manifestation. At times in the guise of 'Dharma', at times in the name of faith and belief and often, in the name of protection of its own cultural existence. After all, communalism wants to keep its existence and dominance intact. This situation would continue until a real transformation of the inner-self of mankind takes place. This real transformation of inner-self does not mean rejection of new thoughts in the outer world or forced imposition of some specific beliefs for transformation. Forced imposition of any system with the help of the outer world can neither enlighten the inner-self nor transform it. This transformation has to be brought about by the person himself. He himself only would have to use deep realisation of his inner-self to explore the means for the transformation. Externally, the most that can be done is to provide ideological freedom to a person for attacking superstition, hypocrisy and sophism. Venomous creepers of communalism have not flourished in civilisations where development of ideological freedom has been provided full respect. Only opportunities for and development of ideological freedom provide maximum help in transformation of the inner-self. We need to take care that when we talk of ideological

Existence oftolerance and liberality along with communalism is impossible. Once communalism creates its space,it makes al l possible efforts for its expansion. Communalism cannot be kept in control for long just on the strength of power and law.

freedom and give respect to it. We should not be doing anything that looks unfavourable to us for ourselves under similar circumstances. It is one thing to contradict others' thoughts and it is entirely different to crush it and impose our ideological sovereignty on others. The main idea of the right to ideological freedom is that we should learn to respect other's thoughts even when contradicting it. There is at all no place here for any feelings of exploitation or victimisation of any person on the basis of ideological differences. Providing respect to ideological differences does not make communalism flourish. Instead, the main reason for emergence of communalism is the ideological fanaticism that has no place for other thoughts and ideological freedom. The more this ideological fanaticism, the more would be intolerance and communalism.

Communalism and intolerance are two sides of the same coin. Both instincts are fully dependent on each other and are also helpful in development of each other. When a person becomes too violent to safeguard his thoughts, beliefs and traditions, he becomes intolerant and unkind towards others' thoughts and beliefs. This egocentric intolerance and violence pushes him towards bloodshed and destruction. The battles and bloodshed taking place in the name of 'Dharma' are all results of this very mentality. This intolerance is adopted sometimes in the name of protecting oneself and sometimes in the name of publicising and propagating some of one's own specific thoughts. One thing is clear that once a person or organisation or community or group makes use of intolerance, he or it first of all becomes violent and then slowly this violence turns into hysteria. Where there is intolerance, violence and hysteria, there can never be peace, cordiality and brotherhood. In such circumstances, if any side becomes too idealistic, talks of liberality, brotherhood and cordiality and does not retaliate the attacks mounted by fanatics, that side would be annihilated Humility is a virtue, liberality is a benignancy; but too much of liberality, humility, and tolerance

Communalism and intolerance are two sides of the same coin. Both instincts are fully dependent on each other and are also helpful in development of each other. When a person becomes too violent to safeguard his thoughts, beliefs and traditions.

ultimately becomes the reason for destruction. A person should be thoroughly liberal and tolerant in his life, but only to the extent that his self and his own existence is not in danger. Those civilisations and cultures that have understood and adopted this psychology have always been able to protect themselves from external attacks. The attacks mounted for establishment of ideological sovereignty are replete with treachery; hence a lot of caution is required in such cases. Humans have linked safeguarding of 'conventional Dharma' and its enrichment with the right of freedom of thoughts, faiths and beliefs and thus, indirectly, even intolerance and treachery have got acceptance. Encouraging mankind to embrace complete liberality, tolerance and brotherhood and attaining peace in this world are serious issues in this age of transition.

Humans have linked safeguarding of 'conventional Dharma' and its enrichment with the right of freedom of thoughts, faiths and beliefs and thus, indirectly, even intolerance and treachery have got acceptance.

When we discuss on Dharma, we should also understand that at ground level, the age of 'Param Dharma' is yet to come. In the age of Param Dharma, the inner-self of a person would not be eclipsed by depravity and there would not be any intolerance, fanaticism and illiberality there. The inner-self of a person would have undergone complete transformation in the age of Param Dharma; but the present situation is not like that. Time and again, such humans keep on incarnating on this earth and we call them incarnations or great personas, whose inner-selves are fully enlightened. Fully enlightened inner-self means that which is filled with complete selflessness and **unassumingness for welfare, being dedicated fully towards supreme oneness. Such a person is a 'complete human' in real sense; but until a person conquers his animal instincts completely, status of 'complete human' would not be available in general.**

A 'complete human' means a person devoid of communal consciousness. But, the existence of 'complete human' is not a reality today. We all are surely making efforts to become complete humans but still have not attained the status or have got transformed into 'complete humans'. Spirituality and righteousness help us in moving towards the status of complete humans. However, it may take us quite some time to become complete considering the kind of divided righteousness being used and the half-hearted way righteous life is being lived currently. Though, it is true that ultimately, every creature would get completeness, as that is the destiny of 'Dharmachakra' i.e. development-cycle; but, even the reality of the present cannot be ignored. In the development-process of mankind, 'complete man' have certainly been incarnating time and again and may be appearing in future also. Their lives and thoughts are just a direction-pointer and symbolic torchbearer for us. Indications of a 'complete man' are generally mysterious, as such a person performs his duties remaining in the consciousness of *virat* (i.e. Bramha) and non-duality. There is no communal approach and partiality in his life and action. Not only liberality, equality, totality, fraternity, love, kindness and non-violence are parts of his nature. He also becomes the personification of these divine values or their colossal form depending on the place, time and circumstances. We find such a demigod in different forms in different periods. A certain demigod is the personification of totality, another is fraternity incarnate and still another, the personification of supreme love, non-violence and kindness. This process of development is extremely mysterious. This touch of completeness cannot be understood fully by any person ever. Till the time a feeling of being a realiser or being a witness exists, even a bit of incompleteness in whatever form would continue to surely exist. He who wants to experience completeness would have to forego the feeling of experiencer also. It may be presumed that then only truth would be reachable. But, such a situation is not possible while living in this world. Communalism exists, at least in minute form, till the time a feeling of the world exists or existence of mind is there. Though we may call this type of communalism as 'moral communalism', there are many dangers here also and the biggest danger is that the claim

Spirituality and righteousness helpus in moving towards the status ofcomplete humans. However,it may take us quite some time to become complete considering the kind ofdivided righteousness being used.

of 'moral communalism' can be made only in the form of hypocrisy. Hence, it may be said on the basis of presumption that 'moral communalism' would ultimately and surely take an egocentric form. And very entry of ego and self-interest would make communalism relinquish its complete morality and finally the person would move towards *rajas* and *tamas*. This situation cannot be treated as moving ahead or development, rather this can be referred to as degeneration or decline only.

One question that gets raised time and again in today's society is- how much is 'Dharma' related to communalism? Answer to this may be given in both the ways. Dharma in its form of totality, completeness, *rit* (ऋत) and truth can never be communal. In its total form, there is no reason for it to be narrow-minded and partial or give a feeling of separation. Complete Chaitanya-centred Dharma has no relation with partiality and perversity. Indian philosophers have understood '*Rit* Dharma' in this form only. However, this form of Dharma cannot be referred to as religion, cult, mazahab or sect. Eternal Dharma is quite different from religion, cult, mazahab, sect or faith. But the situation changes when we view 'Dharma' in a divided form because of divided consciousness. This division of 'Dharma' diverts us towards communalism. 'Dharma' based on divided consciousness would be parochial and even pertinacious. This pertinacity may be called sometimes as 'perseverance' and sometimes as 'perversity'. In common words, 'communalism' comes into play once we add to Dharma our analysis based on our contemplation and faith. If Dharma is Hindu or Muslim or Jew or Jain or Buddhist or Christian, it is communal. And when Dharma turns communal, the first negative effect is that 'righteousness' starts getting insignificant and 'rituals' and vested self-interest start getting importance. The real value in the society is that of righteousness, as making righteousness communal is impossible. Righteousness can never be communal just as light can never be communal. Righteousness in itself is energy i.e. light; there is no chance at all of it being communal.

However, this form of Dharma cannot be referred to as religion, cult, mazahab or sect. Eternal Dharma is quite different from religion, cult, mazahab, sect or faith. But the situation changes when we view 'Dharma' in a divided form.

Thus, today's man does not need Dharma presented in a divided form, instead, he needs righteousness. This righteousness only would take him to divinity. He would be able to ultimately attain peace and happiness only through righteousness. Righteousness only would help remove divisions and streams of love would flow towards each other all around.

Righteousness is a fundamental revolution. It takes us far away from communalism. Righteousness is such a consciousness that aims for awakening of inner-self, illumination of inner-self and transformation of inner-self. Communalism does not transform inner-self, rather which makes inner-self further divided. The existence of separation facilitates habitation and enrichment of communalism, whereas, righteousness cannot at all have any connection with it. Righteousness is in itself complete and monolithic - just like light, just like a flame. It is colossal and all-pervading also like sky. All the Dharma-promoters till date have always relinquished narrow-mindedness and embraced broad-mindedness. In the guise of these Dharma-promoters, however people formed many organisations and abandoned broad-mindedness. The truth is that any organisation cannot ever be broad-minded and monolithic. An organisation on its own creates borders for itself, erects walls and strengthens its perimeters. If borders are not created, the organisation itself would not be formed. There is no organisation for the infinite. There is no way to organise infinite. Supreme liberality, supreme love and the feeling of common-good have nothing to do with organisation. An organisation only talks of the welfare of its own and its members. It believes that only they, who are with the organisation, are correct, dear and respectable. And they, who are not with the organisation, are confused, unworthy and unlikable - such a person can at most be just pitiable. Any organisation formed on the basis of Dharma does not give the status of saint to anybody other than its members. Such organisations

It takes us far away from communalism. Righteousness is such a consciousness that aims for awakening of inner-self, il lumination of inner-self and transformation of inner-self.

are intolerant towards their opponents. They generally keep away from them and even mock their opponents. Hence, such organisations cannot be friendly with each other; rather, they are opponents of each other by nature. Thus it is clear that the organisations formed in the name of Dharma are communal in some or other sense at some or other level. No organisation can be free from communalism. That is the reason that Indian philosophers of the era of Vedanta and Upanishads never created any organisation or association or union in the name of Dharma or for the purpose of spiritual path. Indian philosophers only explored their inner-self and could not even give a name for this awakening of the inner-self, and made this clear announcement that every person would have to walk alone, silently only, on the path of spirituality. The seeker would have to get all experiences himself; experiences of others would not work for him. All the explorations would have to be done alone. Answers to questions would have to be found on one's own. Still more important than getting answers is that one has to live every moment as per his thoughts. No question should be raised; rather, one has to keep himself calm. All the explorations have to be made inside, as there is nothing outside. The experiences of even the greatest of great Dharma-promoters can be at most some hazy indications and some incomplete signals. Hence, one has to look for his path on his own and also walk on it alone. Nobody else can provide a company in this exploration of inner-self. This is the reason that Bhagavan Buddha, while on his deathbed, had said in his last advice to his greatest disciple Ananda - 'Appo Deepo Bhava' i.e. be a light unto yourself. But the followers of Buddha rejected this last advice. They formed their organisation, the *sangha* and on their own, tied their feet with the shackles of narrow-mindedness. They did not go into their inner-self to explore Dharma. They went to the *sangha*. These followers did not look inside; instead, they sought external help. Exploration of Dharma is an exploration of the inner-self; how can Dharma be attained

They generally keep away from them and even mock their opponents. Hence, such organisations cannot be friendly with each other; rather, they are opponents of each other by nature.

by exploring outside? Something similar, as the disciples and followers of Buddha had done, was done by the followers of Rama and Krishna, devotees of Shankar, also by the disciples and followers of Christ and Nanak. The followers of Muhammad formed similar fanatic organisations and linked righteous consciousness with arrogance and intolerance. Thus, all those who connected with their spiritual heads made them communal instead of making them *virat* (Bramha). The spiritual heads had actually incarnated this form for the benefit of humanity. They actually taught liberality, tolerance, compassion, love, kindness and non-violence; they demolished all the walls of separation. But, the disciples and followers of those spiritual heads erected the walls of separation and even made them stronger. Because of this narrow-mindedness, righteousness was not nourished in the world; instead, communalism was more nourished. Self-interest was linked to this communalism and is still linked. Communalism is a source of gratification for arrogance. Mahatma Buddha, Mahavira, Christ, Guru Nanak Dev Ji and even Adi Shankar Ji never provided gratification to arrogance. They did not create any shroud of principles; they did not stipulate any constraints of words; rather, these demigods tried to free the mind from bonds. These demigods, who are known as Dharma-promoters, never announced in their life that they have come to establish any new Dharma. Their attempt was that the people, living in the society where they lived, should have clean behaviour with no credibility gap and there should be no ignorance. How can the attempt to remove ignorance be called communal? Communalism in itself is ignorance, darkness and such a vice that promotes discords, unrest, exploitation, injustice and bloodshed.

For world peace, communalism would have to be given up. All those shops running in the name of Dharma would have to be boycotted. We would have to remain ever careful of the poison of divisions in the name of Dharma.

For world peace, communalism would have to be given up. All those shops running in the name of Dharma would have to be boycotted. We would have to remain ever careful of the poison of divisions in the name of Dharma. New measures would have to be explored to prevent these divisions, separation and partitions from turning us communal. We may or may not eliminate the organisations created in the name of Dharma, but we may at least ensure that no organisation is allowed to have a right to impose its ideology on others using money power or deceit or muscle power. Today, the organisations formed in the name of Dharma are raising the walls of division or separation in the guise of publicising their ideology. Whereas, nothing should be allowed, in the guise of making mankind more civilised and cultured, that raises the walls of separation further and makes the same stronger. Today's man can at least ensure to have a system where such organisations do not become a hindrance to the development of human prudence. And do not create hurdles, in the guise of right of devotion, faith and belief, to the development of intelligence and rationality.

We would have to remain ever careful of the poison of divisions in the name of Dharma. New measures would have to be explored to prevent these divisions, separation and partitions from turning us communal.

Today, the biggest concern is that what we are referring to as 'Dharma' is just another form of communalism. It may be contextual and appropriate to mention here that the world cannot enter supreme oneness with the existence of 'divided consciousness'. However, Dharma is the medium that is related to the development of humans that aims for attainment of supreme oneness. There is no communalism in Dharma but communalism may have some degree of Dharma. Even a minute fragment of Dharma provides communalism at least some beauty, relevance and prosperity. The West has assumed this very prosperity as the goal of Dharma. Thus, this very prosperity linked to communal pertinacity has become the focal point for the Western mind. To provide honour to their current situation, the West has started addressing this very communal consciousness as Dharma. Now, philosophers of the West are slowly succeeding in imposing this narrow definition of Dharma on the world with the help of their monetary and publicity powers. Indian philosophy completely rejects this interpretation of Dharma; but communalism, wearing the robe of Dharma, has become so powerful that it is not able to understand Indian thinking. Currently, the situation across the globe is that religious fanaticism that can be commonly called as communal fanaticism is growing. This very fanaticism is turning into a curse for humanity - sometime as hysteria and sometime as intolerance-centric mania. Under some circumstances, this communalism is not only violent but extremely violent and has exceeded the limits of brutality. The unfortunate thing is that even today, when man is comparatively more civilised, cultured, intelligent and rationalist, he does not want to expunge those pieces. And this, from the so called religious scriptures that are not only fanatic in nature but brutal as well. It is surprising that at present, the civilised and cultured man either avoids or ignores to publicly condemn the brutality being inflicted in the name of Dharma.

If peace and civilisation were to be developed in this world, all such thoughts that propagate hatred and intolerance would have to be definitely expunged from these scriptures. If in the guise of religious scriptures, directions like this are issued from the places of worship.

The malpractices being nourished in the guise of Dharma also fall in the same category. It is not a secret how caste system got recognised in the guise of Dharma in Indian life. The way brutal atrocities were inflicted on one class of society because of this caste system can be viewed in the same context. Fortunately, the Indian mind has started to protest against this caste system and all other malpractices and as on date, nobody supports caste system except some isolated conservatives. As far as brutality is concerned, even conservatives do not support it. This is evidence that the Indian society is trying to get rid of communalism. However, there are still innumerable such cultures and ideologies in this world that do not want to free themselves from brutal thinking because of their arrogance, self-interest or their fanaticism. This is a serious issue and there is a need to be careful of this. In today's world, recognising thoughts in religious scriptures that profess hatred towards others and prescribe murder of people following any other faith, just in the name of Dharma, is not justified. If peace and civilisation were to be developed in this world, all such thoughts that propagate hatred and intolerance would have to be definitely expunged from these scriptures. If in the guise of religious scriptures, directions like this are issued from the places of worship -

'O faithful, be aware that idolaters are impure', and if further directions like this are also issued against idolaters - 'When the forbidden month is over, wherever you find idolaters, catch them, corner them and kill them. Look for them and ambush them. Later, if they repent, agree to offer namaj and give alms, let them go'. How can a civilised society permit publicity and propagation of such directions? How can the communities issuing such directions be treated as humanitarian? This is not a correct approach that just because something like this is written in the scripture - 'O faithful, you should not make friends with Jews and Christians', such thinking should get recognition for publicity. Terrorism would flourish and even wars would take place if the entire world does not confront this communal ideology unitedly.

Feelings of enmity, hatred, hostility and acrimony are hurdles in the development of human beings and their co-existence. Humanity would have to be protected from these evil feelings and communalism linked it.

A co-existence with communalism and brutality cannot be recognised just for the sake of co-existence. Similarly, brutality, hostility and hatred cannot be provided recognition by using the principles of '*Sarva Dharma Sama Bhava i.e.* 'All religions are the same' or '*Sarva Dharma Samman i.e.* Honour for all religions'. This would be immorality and injustice. This would be even called insanity. Even where Dharma has multiple concepts and is linked to Hindu, Muslim, Sikh, Christian, Buddhist, Jain, Jew or Parsi, communalism cannot be permitted to use brutality and enmity. Feelings of enmity, hatred, hostility and acrimony are hurdles in the development of human beings and their co-existence. Humanity would have to be protected from these evil feelings and communalism linked it. Then only development of feelings of cordiality and '*Sarva Dharma Sama Bhava' would be possible in this world. 'Sarva Dharma Sama Bhava' is the most needed in the context of co-existence. A situation of 'Sarva Dharma Sama Bhava' is the notion of consciousness of superman. Hence, if we have to live in this world, we would have to come down to the level below that of the feeling of super consciousness. Once below the level of super consciousness, it becomes necessary to oppose communal concepts. Hence, we will have to definitely oppose communalism, fundamentalism and fanaticism. Those who stubbornly wish to still continue with the consciousness of fundamentalism and fanaticism may remain so. When we have a discussion with them, we should gather the courage to declare that we treat fanaticism and communalism as evils and we would not link ourselves with it.*

□

10

Dharma, Politics and Indian Consciousness: Core Values of Indian Life

India is a country brimming with spiritual consciousness. It's here that the concepts of Dharma took birth. It's here that the eternity of Dharma was recognised and it's here that Dharma was given a shape that may be significant for the development of all living beings. However, today, Dharma has been made a synonym to mazahab, panth and 'religion'. What is the justification of linking Dharma to mazahab or rituals in a country where 'truth is Dharma and Dharma is truth' is well-accepted. Also, where the mantra of *'Satyameva Jayate* i.e. truth alone triumphs' has been embraced by all and been recognised as a component of national consciousness? Is this not a grave irony that Dharma has been linked to mazahab and rituals? The motto or the model sentence for Indian constitution and Indian Parliament is '*Dharmachakra Pravartanaay*'. But this feeling is not appearing in that consciousness that is being expressed today. Despite '*Dharmachakra Pravartanaay*' being the ideal for Indian politics and entire Indian politics born out of Dharma, there is hesitation in glorifying the importance of Dharma?

Definitely, Dharma is neither rituals nor hypocrisy and Dharma is also not linked to conservatism. It is a complete transformation in itself. Dharma is the consciousness that teaches ways to rebel against those established values in society that create hurdles in development of all living beings. When Dharma relinquishes this revolutionary consciousness, it becomes either cult or hypocrisy. Dharma is like the burning flame of a lamp that knows how to provide light upward only. The Dharma that does not have the capacity to break customs of society cannot be so, even if anybody continues to address it or name it as Dharma. Some instincts, rituals or any specific consciousness or specific duty may be provided the cloak of Dharma, but that would not make that specific duty or specific consciousness a real Dharma. Real Dharma depends on that mentality which aims not only for welfare of all living beings but also their all-round development.

It's extremely difficult to define Dharma. This has become all the more onerous as the Indian mind has been invaded by Western culture and Western consciousness and it is slowly losing its original ideology. The extent of erosion that Indian consciousness has undergone because of Western philosophy and culture is so severe that it is even forgetting its original character. If it were not so, those misconceptions in respect of Dharma that are visible all across India today, would not have arisen. Not only an average person of the country, but even renowned intellectuals, scholars and philosophers are gripped by these misconceptions. It is an irony that instead of finding a solution to this problem, it is being aggravated only. This problem is growing more serious as Western ideology is dominating Indian consciousness. We have sought criteria from the West only for evaluating ourselves, whereas, despite all the compulsions and erosion, India is still prosperous with all those values that can do well for the whole world. However, the world would accept these values only when, first of all, we Indians adopt it in our lives. Until Indian philosophy and ideology is recognised in its own home, nothing is going to be achieved by shouting and presenting our ideology on international platforms.

It's extremely difficult to define Dharma. This has become all the more onerous as the Indian mind has been invaded by Western culture and Western consciousness and it is slowly losing its original ideology. The extent of erosion that Indian consciousness has undergone.

It's not that spiritual consciousness or righteous consciousness did not get developed in other countries of the world. It did get developed. The development in India has a specialty, and that has come from the affirmation of acceptance of introverted contemplation of consciousness. In the context of Indian consciousness, Dharma may be divided into two parts. One side of Dharma refers to extroverted contemplation and the other side is introverted contemplation. The introverted side of Dharma is eternal, just as the acceptance of one Supreme Being in entire universe. We may call this Supreme Being a soul or even God. This Supreme Being is permanent and all changes are dependent on it and that is the reason that one of the interpretations of Dharma from the Indian point of view is that the very character of any object that proves its existence is its Dharma. Apart from this introverted side, there is also an extroverted side of Dharma that we refer to as conventional Dharma and establish in the form of external behaviour. Concepts like temporal framework of our relationship with each other and a person's Dharma and duties towards another person and Mother Nature are understood with the help of external consciousness. This extroverted side of Dharma keeps on getting impacted by place, time and circumstances. There are many other sides of Dharma like Dharma of a human being, Dharma of family, Dharma of society, Dharma of nation and something connected to it, *Yuga Dharma* i.e. Dharma of an age.

Just like a person has his Dharma, every age also has its Dharma. The existence of Yuga Dharma is eternal, but this eternity of Yuga Dharma does not mean that the duty or the spiritual consciousness that is reasonable for an age would be reasonable for all ages.

Just like a person has his Dharma, every age also has its Dharma. The existence of Yuga Dharma is eternal, but this eternity of Yuga Dharma does not mean that the duty or the spiritual consciousness that is reasonable for an age would be reasonable for all ages. It is changeability that is the life force and character of Yuga Dharma. Just as Nature undergoes changes every moment, Yuga Dharma also gets impacted by time. There is no static existence in the Nature at all; the thing is undergoing either development or erosion every moment. That's why we call Mother Nature capricious. Extroverted consciousness can never be quiet. Whatever comes within the purview of mind, whatever gets affected by the purview of mind becomes the reason for change. That change is the creator of Yuga Dharma. When we cross beyond the consciousness of mind and tear off all the sheaths that cover our consciousness, we enter such an introverted consciousness that is beyond our minds. Only then, we attain peace and happiness. This form of Dharma is born out of that divine spiritual centre that has been defined as the Supreme Being in Indian philosophy. Indian philosophy recognises inanimate object and also Supreme Being that is beyond even *Vigyanmaya Kosha* and *Anandamaya Kosha.* That form of Dharma that takes a person beyond the state of *Anandamaya Kosha,* provides a glimpse of eternal form of Dharma. The world that is even beyond *Anandamaya Kosha* does not have any division. There is Supreme Oneness in that world. There no presence at all of the feeling of duality there; hence this world cannot be expressed in words and even the experiences of this world cannot be chronicled in words. This is the characteristic of Indian philosophy. The West is not able to understand this very characteristic of Indian philosophy, and that is because their thinking is based on extroverted consciousness. It's not that Western philosophers do not have introverted consciousness. They also have introverted consciousness but their ingress into introverted consciousness is limited and very superficial. They could not go much deeper inside.

Indian philosophy recognises inanimate object and also Supreme Being that is beyond even Vigyanmaya Kosha and Anandamaya Kosha. That form of Dharma that takes a person beyond the state of Anandamaya Kosha.

Truth, non-violence, peace, love and goodwill are all components of Dharma and they are dynamic components, not static. Dharma is not an inanimate thing and also not an absolute thing or absolute action or thinking that does not have any eternal basis. In fact, despite having eternal basis, Dharma has dynamism and that is the characteristic of Dharma. The spirit of non-duality is the basis of Dharma and impetus of duality is the dynamic strength of Dharma. The dynamism of Dharma is linked to that transformability that is aimed towards welfare of all creatures and manifestation of that divinity that is born out of non-duality. But this ideology of Indian philosophy is not getting resonated from any platform - not even in Dharma related meetings and conferences. It's so unfortunate that even in the seventh World Religions Conference held in 1994, Dharma was treated as a synonym for 'religion'. Whereas, the word 'religion' does not have the power to express the kind of consciousness that is expressed by the word 'Dharma'. The word 'religion' possesses neither universality nor consciousness of the whole. It also does not possess that dynamism and transformability that is an important basic element of Dharma. Dharma is the carrier of the clarion call raised against conservatism. It is that consciousness that ruptures even established gloom. Dharma is that fire of knowledge whose flames incinerate all those hurdles that do not want to help in the development of all living beings. It is auspicious and dedicated not only to mankind but also to entire inanimate and living beings and entire Mother Nature. It's not clear why our Indian saints, philosophers, thinkers, politicians and eminent persons are not able to present this side of Dharma where they are invited for discussions on Dharma. It's also not clear why they link themselves to a religious mentality and try to understand and help others understand the word 'Dharma' with their narrow-minded viewpoints. After all, how to bring to light the truth that is inherent in the word 'Dharma'? No doubt, that day is sure to come when nobody would be able to stop this truth to come to light.

Dharma is the carrier of the clarion call raised against conservatism. It is that consciousness that ruptures even established gloom. Dharma is that fire of knowledge whose flames incinerate all those hurdles that do not want to helpin.

Even in its extroverted form, Dharma is not a stony or rooted consciousness, rather it is such a consciousness that is perpetually floating and has the capability to fight and grapple with wheel of time and make changes. That which cannot move with the speed of wheel of time is not Dharma and that is the reason, in Indian philosophy, it has never been linked to books or any specific person or any specific spiritual guru. Even the greatest of great Indian seers, philosophers or spiritual gurus do not have the power to be able to establish the fundamental consciousness of Dharma single-handedly. The Indian mind has always adored intelligence and intelligence is not a birth right of any person or spiritual guru. Development of intelligence is eternal. Dharma is also eternal, as Dharma is also born out of intelligence; hence, in this worldly life, this intelligence based transformability of Dharma will have to be accepted. Else Dharma would lose its original character and would get enslaved by conservative ideologies and then interpretations presented by some specific people would start getting recognised as Dharma. The moral values prescribed for running day-to-day life by a person are extremely temporary form of Dharma. Moral values cannot be eternal truth. Moral and social values of the time some five thousand years ago are nowhere visible in our society today. Does it mean that Dharma has changed? If it is interpreted that Dharma has changed, it would lose its eternal character. Hence, it is very much justified that the word 'Dharma' is not shackled by moral values, as when we shackle the word 'Dharma' with moral values, we put something like a stop to it. When stopped, Dharma turns into something like a pond and loses its intellect and power to keep its intelligence dynamic. Real Yuga Dharma is actually a form of the eternally flowing Ganges of intellect, and only the people who know and understand the fundamental nature of this flowing water can see this form. It would be injustice to Dharma to get it constrained by some specific thought, link it to specific ideology, connect it to any specific book or make it dependent on some specific person. In a sense, all these would be a kind of unrighteousness only. There is motion in Dharma and it is eternal motion. Dharma can cross over place, time and circumstances and still maintain its momentum.

in this worldly life, this intelligence based transformability of Dharma will have to be accepted. Else Dharma would lose its original character and would get enslaved by conservative ideologies and then interpretations presented.

As far as politics is concerned, both international and national politics are corrupted by self-interest, narrow-mindedness and arrogance, and Dharma cannot exist where there is arrogance. Dharma has a spirit of devotion towards that divine existence that comes from the world where there is no restraint and hurdle. But, politics does not come from that world. The consciousness of politics has been created for the purpose of supremacy of the self. Self-interest is the main element in the consciousness of politics - be it the self-interest of society or self-interest of mankind or all creatures. Politics cannot be born in the absence of consciousness of self-interest. Politics means recognising the existence of power of morality. Politics is used only for removing the authority of immorality and establishing the authority of morality. In this context, making a reference to the grand saying in Geeta - *'Dharma Sansthapnarthay' (i.e. for proper establishment of Dharma)* would be appropriate.

Swadharma is quite important in politics; but what is this Swadharma? Is this Swadharma unique for each individual? In fact, Swadharma for two persons can never be same, as it is related to the consciousness of a person, his own contemplation and his own nature. Intelligence and rationality of different persons cannot be same; there would certainly be some difference. Hence, every person living in a society would have to define his Dharma himself by exploring his inner-self. The main reason for this difference in intelligence is - uniqueness in desires of each person. A normal creature defines his duty to satisfy his senses and desires or to satisfy the sentiments of his mind or to provide importance to his intelligence. The attachment that a person has towards results of his *karma* is the reason for differences in intelligence in different persons. The same kind of karma creates different kinds of instincts and many kinds of consciousness in different persons; hence, people who want to understand Dharma would have to also realise and understand this form of intelligence remaining unacquisitive, unfazed and unassuming. Until this happens, the real essence of Dharma would remain incomprehensible.

Swadharma is quite important in politics; but what is this Swadharma? Is this Swadharma unique for each individual? In fact,Swadharma for two persons can never be same,as it is related to the consciousness.

Dharma is related to karma and cannot exist without it. They are complementary to each other. When and which karma is treated as unrighteous and when and which one is treated as righteous - this can be decided only on the basis of Yuga Dharma. This cannot be decided by going through books. They, who desire to realise and understand Yuga Dharma, would have to first of all, relinquish their hesitation. In the context of Dharma, hesitation means self-destruction and also destruction of things around us.

When Dharma gets separated from transformation, it relinquishes its fundamental character, and even if people call it Dharma, it becomes, in reality, unrighteousness. Great spiritual guides keep incarnating to demolish this unrighteousness.

If only current Indian politics could have understood this character of Dharma!

If only politics of the world and politicians of the world could have assimilated the real meaning of *'Dharmachakra Pravartanaay'* and recognised the radiance and transformability of Dharma!

Until that happens, mankind would remain slave to customs. Yuga Dharma aims for making us free from customs and Yuga Dharma only is ultimately the wish of all living beings. Here, this needs to be understood clearly that the entire strength of politics lies in its creativity only, and this very creativity is the transformability of politics. On a worldly level, both politics and Dharma are in favour of creative transformation, and hence in this context, they are also complementary to each other.

□

11

Understand the Essence of Dharma

It's difficult to understand why there are talks of separating Dharma from politics without properly defining it. The word 'Dharma' has several meanings in the context of Indian culture and philosophy. As per the basic meaning of word 'Dharma', that which proves the existence of an object is the fundamental Dharma of that object. However, the word 'Dharma' has been used with several meanings other than this. That is the reason that Dharma also refers to duty, humanitarian principles and even consciousness of welfare for all. In due course, misuse of this word resulted in linking of Dharma with rituals and the word 'Dharma' became a symbol of conservatism, religious obsession, sect, panth and faith. In fact, this is the reason that today, there are misconceptions all around with regard to the word 'Dharma'. The society today is in a state of delusion. Until the word 'Dharma' is provided a clear definition to remove this delusion, any attempt to separate this word from politics would be just a joke and a show of political malice.

Tragedy of 6 December

Whatever happened on 6 December 1992 was a very unfortunate incident. And Bharatiya Janata Party had to pay the price for that incident. But nothing such happened on 6 December that should prompt us to believe that the constitution of our country is going to be dilapidated now and even foundation stones of secularism are going to be demolished. Whereas an indirect contempt of Supreme Court did take place on 6 December, the assurance that Bharatiya Janata Party had given to the country was also broken and national psyche was badly bruised. This unfortunate incident also brought to light some pertinent facts and it would not be proper to ignore them. The most important fact that came to light is that national sentiments cannot be kept suppressed for long by political manoeuvres. When there is too much of political manoeuvring in the context of national sentiments, the impatient general public revolts, as happened in Ayodhya on 6 December. Ultimately, the fact that came to light after the incident of 6 December is that alien invaders had constructed a mosque by demolishing the temple standing at the birthplace of Rama. And the purpose of building that mosque was not to offer prayers to their Lord but only to impinge on Indian culture, overrun the Indian soul and crush the pride of national consciousness. This misdeed of alien invaders cannot be linked to national pride. The explosion of people's emotions in Ayodhya on 6 December took place only because national pride was being eroded. And also, national identity was being disrespected and Indian government was ignoring the feelings and aspirations of people. This is of course correct that the way that disputed structure was demolished was unfair and unconstitutional. Such destruction should not have taken place. This is also true that sometimes destruction brings to light such facts that ultimately become very helpful in nation building. Destruction is certainly devastating, but every destruction has some or other process of construction hidden in itself.

The explosion of people's emotions in Ayodhya on 6 December took place only because national pride was being eroded. And also, national identity was being disrespected and Indian government was ignoring the feelings and aspirations of people.

Dharma and Morality

If anybody does not want to think over Dharma honestly, he should at least agree to the thoughts of Gandhi. Gandhi did not recognise any difference between Dharma and morality and used to always say that Dharma and morality were synonyms to each other and could be used in place of each other. Gandhi had acquired the foundations of Dharma from Upanishads. According to Gandhi, Hindu customs and traditions were rituals and they did not have any relation with Dharma. Gandhi mentioned this on many occasions that he did not use the word Dharma with the meaning that is understood today. He used Dharma in the same sense that was used by Indian seers and sages in ancient times. Gandhi used to say that Dharma should be certainly present in each of our instincts. He had also said that we should seek guidance for all our instincts only through it. According to him, Dharma helps a person in every aspect and truth only is Dharma, truth only is the supreme God and truth can be realised and understood only by following the rules of morality. It's difficult to understand why politicians and specially Congressmen today do not want to follow the path suggested by Gandhi. Today, it appears that Congress wants to renounce the philosophy that was presented by Gandhi through his prayer meetings. Perhaps this is happening because Congress is afraid of Bharatiya Janata Party. It was for mere political gains that they purposefully mis-represented the word 'Dharma' and bring in a legislation that would have only increased misconceptions and aggravated discords. This is a fact that this legislation could not be passed in Parliament, but the accusations that were leveled against Congress with regard to this legislation have not been responded till date. But Congress would have to ultimately respond. The party would have to clarify what they mean by the word 'Dharma'. If they treat Dharma as mazahab, faith or sect, then the matter would be different. Definitely, politics cannot be chained with shackles of communalism. Rituals and religious conservatism are not desirables for Indian politics. Indian politics would have to be separated from mosques, gurudwaras, churches, monasteries and temples. This should not happen that fatwas from mosques and pronouncements from churches and edicts from gurudwaras are obtained for influencing voters. If interference is made by the places of prayer in politics, not only Indian politics would be blemished but this degenerate and demolish our ideals that are the backbone of Indian culture. Hence, we will have to ponder in what sense we are using the word 'Dharma' and

If they treat Dharma as mazahab, faith or sect, then the matter would be different. Definitely, politics cannot be chained with shackles of communalism. Rituals and religious conservatism are not desirables for Indian politics.

what should be its real meaning. Unfortunately, without understanding the mysteries of Dharma, today's politics is being run through mosques, churches and gurudwaras. States like Mizoram and Nagaland are already in the grasp of churches and Indian culture and Indian philosophy are openly being denigrated in these states. If only the entire country could be made aware of the actual points of view of Indian philosophers in respect of Dharma! If we connect ourselves with the nation's mainstream culture and proclaim that all religious conservatism have no place here, we would appreciate the core value of Indian culture. That core principle conveys - 'सर्वभूत हितेरत:' ('*Sarvabhut Hiteratah*') and 'may there be welfare for all'. There should be welfare not only for Hindus but even Sikhs, Christians, Muslims and Buddhists. May there be welfare for those who are theist and also for those who are atheist. This spirit of welfare for all is available only in Indian philosophy and this can be attained only through Indian culture. However, under current circumstances, this can be attained only when we define and establish Dharma in the form in which it has been defined in Indian Upanishads. It's not clear why Indian politics is having objection in accepting this appropriate and correct definition having the spirit of common good. We do not have to connect ourselves to any set of rituals; instead, we should connect to the knowledge store of Indian culture.

States like Mizoram and Nagaland are already in the grasp of churches and Indian culture and Indian philosophy are openly being denigrated in these states. If only the entire country could be made aware of the actual points of view of Indian philosophers

श्रृण्वन्तु विश्वे अमृतस्य पुत्राः
आ ये धामानि दिव्यानि तस्थुः
वेदाहमेतं पुरुषं महतं
आदित्यवर्णं तमसा परस्तात्।

(i.e. Listen, O children of immortality the world over. You have attained divine truth that is majestic like the Sun. Realise and understand it.)

This Vedic proclamation is not meant only for those living in India but also for those living all around the world. According to this, every male and female living on this earth is the son or daughter of immortality i.e. they are divine souls. There is nothing non-divine here, such was the feeling of those philosophers who had realised and understood the fundamental character of Dharma.

Dharma and Swadharma

Just like his breadth, Dharma is linked to every component of a person's life in the same form in which it has been defined in Upanishads. Rashtra-Dharma, Maanav-Dharma, Putra-Dharma, Pitri-Dharma, Matri-Dharma, Guru-Dharma, etc. are not related to Hindu, Muslim or Christian Dharma. According to the people who follow Indian culture, Hindu, Muslim and Christian are not Dharmas rather they are faiths. People who call themselves knowledgeable about Indian philosophy are not able to accept this because of their immature thinking. They have divided Dharma and then started calling Hindu Dharma, Christian Dharma and Muslim Dharma. Dharma cannot be divided. Even in the form of swadharma, it is completely whole, though swadharma has a special meaning. Swadharma means those duties that are based on a person's own culture and his inborn interests. In this context, one Indian hermit has written in his book 'Geeta Tatva Chintan', "If a couple has ten children, swadharma of all those children would be different from each other." This is because each of them would have a different culture and different character. Some of them may become businessmen, some may become doctors and others become writers. Some may like specific food and others may like other food and these very differences in their character would determine their life-goals and duties.

Just like his breadth, Dharma is linked to every component of a person's life in the same form in which it has been defined in Upanishads. Rashtra-Dharma, Maanav-Dharma, Putra-Dharma, Pitri-Dharma, Matri-Dharma, Guru-Dharma, etc.

Connecting inborn interests and mental propensities with inner world and spirituality only is called swadharma. Swadharma is helpful in gradual transformation and development as real duty and swadharma are synonyms to each other. But, today, who would understand this spirit of Indian culture? There is a supreme spirit inherent in the word 'Dharma'. The politicians of today do not have time to realise and understand it in that form, hence everything is falling apart and everything is disintegrating. When Bhishma was on his deathbed, he had advised to follow Dharma. He did not advise any rituals. He had said, "आत्मनः प्रतिकूलानि परेषां न समाचारेत" meaning, 'Do not do anything that you treat inimical to yourself'.

Gandhi's Dharma

The Gita was dear to Gandhi and his philosophy of life was the same as that formulated by the Gita. But, can this philosophy of the Gita become the philosophy of life for Congressmen and other politicians today? Gandhi wished that the philosophy of life articulated by the Gita should be prevalent all around the world. He did not treat the Gita as any religious book. He knew the Gita as a philosophical scripture and he had experimented adopting the truth conveyed by the Gita in his life. He just passed on the facts that came to light out of those experiments, to the society; but, today, all these things have become contradictory to Indian politics. At least, Congress should reply why the situation has come to this state. At least, national philosophy and philosophy of life as formulated by Gandhi cannot be called communal. And if the philosophy of life, national philosophy and political philosophy formulated by Gandhi are not communal, why is there hesitation in adopting them? Why are we not ready to establish the word 'Dharma' in the same form in which Gandhi realised and understood it? 'धर्मो धारयते प्रजाः' ('*dharmo dhaarayate prajah*') - this was the spirit in the mind of Gandhi. He was of the view that a human becomes animal in the absence of Dharma. The sole path of 'अभ्युदय निःश्रेयस' ('*abhyudaya nihshreyas*') is Dharma only and there are four *purusharthas* (objects of human pursuit) for a human being in Indian culture viz. Dharma, artha, kama and moksha. The aim of life should only be to fight back unrighteousness - this was also the spirit of Gandhi, and in his view, British were unrighteous towards India and hence he fought against them. However, today, the

The Gita was dear to Gandhi and his philosophy of life was the same as that formulated by the Gita. But, can this philosophy of the Gita become the philosophy of life for Congressmen and other politicians today?

word 'Dharma' is treated as a symbol of communalism and it is said that whoever talks of Dharma would be declared as communal. This thinking is not correct. This thinking would create a lot of problems for the nation.

Country's Misfortune

Who is not aware that the piece of poetry that Congress had espoused in 1923 was–

'विजयी विश्व तिरंगा प्यारा, झंडा ऊँचा रहे हमारा

×××

आओ प्यारे वीरो आओ, देश, धर्म पर बलि बलि जाओ'

Has Congress now forgotten its own promise that it had made to the country or forgotten the clarion call that it had given to the country? If it has really forgotten, why so? If Congress has really forgotten this, it would not only be their misfortune, but that of the nation and politics, as well. It would be a grave omen.

Animosity, violence, lawlessness and bitterness - finding remedy to all of them and eradicating them only is the Dharma of a government. Fighting communalism is the Dharma of every noble citizen.

As far as communalism is concerned, it has no relation with Dharma at all. As far as caste enmity is concerned, that also has no relation with Dharma at all. Animosity, violence, lawlessness and bitterness - finding remedy to all of them and eradicating them only is the Dharma of a government. Fighting communalism is the Dharma of every noble citizen. Jumping in the battle for defeating the demon of communalism is a crusade; but today, this very spirit is required to be imbibed in real terms. Dharma is certainly not meant only for saffron-robed individuals. Only saffron-robed individuals are not contractors of Dharma, and it's also not correct to assume only they have the right to define Dharma. It's also not right that only Hindus would define or interpret Dharma. Any humanitarian can provide a right definition of Dharma and experience it, as a Hindu or Muslim or Sikh or Christian or Buddhist or Jain. In the context of general daily routines, Dharma means morality. Morality and Dharma are synonymous. Dharma means humanity. Dharma means love. Dharma means truth.

□

12

Dharma and Nation

What is Dharma? Great commentaries may be written on this subject and even a terse definition may be provided for it. A terse definition is - 'धारयते इति धर्मः' (*'dharayate iti Dharmah'*) i.e. that which can be adopted, which helps in development and which provides safety is Dharma. Another brief definition is - that which provides temporal welfare for a person, helps in his advancement and awakens his spiritual consciousness is also Dharma. Dharma is tied with morality. A behaviour without morality cannot be called so. In other words, that which damages morality or which is a cause for loss of morality is not Dharma. Dharma is nourisher of a person, society, nation and humanity and not a destroyer. There is certainly some element of destruction in Dharma, but that is meant for Lord Shiva only. That which is Shiva is divine. That which helps in welfare and development of society is Dharma. There should be welfare for humanity in general and not for any specific community - this is the speciality of Indian culture and Indian philosophy. And this is the Brahmasutra of *'Tatvamasi' (i.e. thou art that). This only is Vedanta and this only is Vedic voice. Human mind resides in higher consciousness and also in lower consciousness. Whatever is born out of lower consciousness contains self-interest, arrogance, narrow-mindedness, conservatism and attachment. This kind of consciousness does help growth in things like sensual satisfaction, material prosperity, etc. but does not provide mental peace and help in blooming of divinity. Whatever is born out of supreme consciousness or higher consciousness contains only liberality and feeling of common good. There is nothing adverse in it; rather it has only compatibility and transcendental self-realisation.*

In this context, it may be said that India and especially Hindu society does not now need transcendental self-realisation, as that does not relate to practical world. The Vedanta philosophy does not change its spirit with change in circumstances. This is correct that the emotion of supreme consciousness cannot be realised by the mind in normal consciousness. In other words, transcendental experience cannot be attained while remaining in lower consciousness, physical consciousness or sensory consciousness. However, we are here not referring to the experience of a transcendental feeling. Rather, we are deliberating on the issue as to what can provide welfare for society and what can provide security for nation. We would like to talk about the nation, which is almost unconscious for the last hundreds of years. The nation whose consciousness is almost lost and which is even today lying in such a state of degeneration where there is neither self-esteem nor national pride. Practical side cannot be ignored for safeguarding self-esteem and awakening national consciousness and that is why the philosophy of life has been propounded in four divisions. These four divisions are Dharma, Artha, Kama and Moksha. Purushartha has a value and that should be definitely made a part of our life. Those setting our house on fire in the name of safeguarding purushartha and national pride would not be appropriate. The first of the four purusharthas is *Dharma* i.e. righteous karma. That which is righteous karma is *Dharma*. That which is unrighteous, that is to say that which should not be done, is not it. This can also be interpreted as duty-bound karma. Duty-bound karma is the real soul of *Dharma*. Duty-bound karma helps earn *Artha*. Duty-bound karma only helps attain material prosperity. Purushartha in the form of *Artha* is the symbol of that material prosperity that generates consciousness of wealth and dignity and can be attained while performing duty-bound karma. The purpose of this material prosperity is the fulfillment of desires. The third purushartha can be attained only after securing prosperity and

The nation whose consciousness is almost lost and which is even today lying in such a state of degeneration where there is neither self-esteem nor national pride. Practical side cannot be ignored for safeguarding self-esteem.

dignity. This very third purushartha is Kama. Desires are fulfilled only by materiality and once senses are satisfied internally, desires dissipate or disappear and the moment of desires disappear, the person attains fourth purushartha. Absolute quenching of desires, perfect peace and complete disappearance of desires is Moksha. Freedom from desires is the core value of the fourth purushartha.

Attack on Indian Philosophy

Our enemies now want to defeat us conclusively. Indian philosophy has been attacked mostly by cultural and ideological storm emanating from the West. Islam also has come from the West. In the real sense, Islam is an extroverted philosophy. It is linked to the body and the material world. Indian philosophy is not concerned only with body and material world but also provides interpretation for the transcendental spirit and that's why it is introverted. But the question here is how much should we embrace out of all that has come from the West, how much should we reject, and why should we embrace or reject. If these questions were to be answered very briefly, the answers would be whatever we think or do should have the spirit of welfare for the world and spirit of national pride. It is not proper to digress and attempt to reach the top by making a jump. Vedanta is the ladder for ultimate development of mankind and sensory pleasure is one of the first steps of human development. Without taking the first step, we cannot reach the last one just by taking a leap. We will have to take the first step and develop ourselves. Development of society and humanity is the next step. Talking of development of humanity without actually developing ourselves would be hypocrisy. The saint society has to ponder how much connected they want to keep themselves with Vedanta i.e. Indian philosophy, and how much disconnected. Even if we do not talk of pure non-dualist Vedanta and remain in the spirit of dualism, everybody would find this thought fully reasonable that there

Our enemies now want to defeat us conclusively. Indian philosophy has been attacked mostly by cultural and ideological storm emanating from the West. Islam also has come from the West. In the real sense, Islam is an extroverted philosophy.

are many ways to reach the Supreme Being. It would not be proper to generate hatred and animosity between individuals just based on the differences in their worship systems. The fact of the matter is, Indian culture does accept the differences in worship systems and that is the reason that even followers of Islam become part of Indian philosophy. Many people, currently, believe that every person living in India is Hindu only, irrespective of the worship system he follows and accordingly, followers of Islam are *Muhammadiyah* Hindus. It is a different matter that followers of Islam in India do not consider themselves Hindu. Who is Hindu and who is not? This has not been clearly explained till now and it also does not appear to be possible till the existence of current political and cultural perversities. Vishva Hindu Parishad has also not provided any clear interpretation of it. In this regard, it would be appropriate to treat every such individual as Hindu who considers himself to be Hindu, as the persons who are against Vedas are also part of great Hindu society. All Jains, Buddhists are also Hindus. Charvaka, who was against Vedas, was also considered a great philosopher in India, and whatever he said was treated as a sacred scripture. Not only that, even the person who opposed Vedas came to be called as God and was treated as an incarnation of Vishnu. No doubt, such a country must be treated as open-minded. Being open-minded does not mean that we should become non-pragmatic. Being pragmatic means safeguarding beliefs and principles and safeguarding them until it appears that too much of reasoning would hurt those beliefs and principles. Knowledge cannot be attained only on the basis of reasoning. That is why, too much of reasoning is called absurdity. This is very unfortunate that today, only such kinds of reasoning too much or absurd reasoning are being presented in the context of Indian pride and Indian soul. Definitely, alien invaders did injustice to India, trod its pride under their feet and made evil attempts to corrupt its culture, and marks of all of them are

It would not be proper to generate hatred and animosity between individuals just based on the differences in their worshipsystems. The fact ofthe matter is,Indian culture does accept the differences in worship systems.

strewn all over India even today. One of them is the place of birth of Shri Ram. Many derogatory blemishes like that are there on our soul and we have to erase all such blemishes. A person who connects his soul and consciousness with those of alien invaders is not a true Indian. Only such a person would be considered a true Indian who is not willing to link himself to alien invaders and enemies of nation. Instead, he connects himself with national pride, philosophy, the mainstream and ancestors of the nation. Muslim worship system is not a hurdle in doing this. Yes, politics is surely a hurdle.

Self-opposing Politics

Jawaharlal Nehru's mind-set was born out of consciousness that had emerged from Western philosophy. He has given a lot to this country and hence the country would remain indebted to him.

It is the country's misfortune that, after independence, no attempt was made to awaken national consciousness and no concrete plan was made to restore the symbols of national pride. If Sardar Patel were alive, he could have probably done something or if Dr. Rajendra Prasad were alive, he would have exerted some pressure for this. However, both of them have left for the heavenly abode. After they left, it appeared as if some void was created in Indian politics. As nothing remains void in Nature, that void was filled up by Jawaharlal Nehru. Jawaharlal Nehru's mind-set was born out of consciousness that had emerged from Western philosophy. He has given a lot to this country and hence the country would remain indebted to him. At the same time, Nehru also did grave injustice to this country. His foremost injustice was that he tried to impose the consciousness born out of the West on Indians. It may be a different issue whether he did this knowingly or unknowingly. Incidentally, Nehru did not have any knowledge of Indian culture and philosophy. He did not understand those finer details that are the foundation stones of Indian philosophy. This very ignorance of his has led Indian politics to such a path that, despite being Indian, is non-Indian.

Unfortunately, Indian politics of date has become self-opposing, following the path suggested by Nehru. This has to be revived, but revival cannot be done by hurting dignity and honour. Where our nation's honour is derived from and where from it is flowing - these are the issues that our philosophers and politicians are required to deliberate on. Can 'Dharma' be interpreted by ignoring things like vision of nation and its practical aspect? Any interpretation made by ignoring the facts and practical aspects cannot be beneficial for society in the real sense. The practical aspect is that when India became independent after the British occupation, it recognised a constitution to get politically streamlined. This constitution is acceptable to all of us even today. If we have to work within this constitution, we would have to take into account its importance and its principles. By ignoring the principles of constitution and trampling over it, we would be dishonouring, disrespecting, slandering and even harming ourselves only. Hence, it is the Dharma of every citizen to follow the path as prescribed by the constitution. The people who do not want to link themselves with the Indian constitution should dissociate themselves from it, say so openly and declare that they want to be separate. Such a situation is not existing today. It is thus clear that we have to safeguard the honour of Indian constitution while also safeguarding the national pride. National pride is not separate from the pride of Hindus and pride of Indian constitution.

The practical aspect is that when India became independent after the British occupation,it recognised a constitution to get politicall y streamlined. This constitution is acceptable to al l ofus even today.

Nation's Honour

Where the Indian flag is disrespected, where the Indian constitution is disrespected, Hindus also would be disrespected there. A Hindu, Muslim, Sikh, Christian or a person following any other faith or any other citizen cannot safeguard his honour separating himself from the nation's honour. Hence, any such action cannot be called righteous. This thought has been presented multiple times in the legendary scriptures of India. As per legendary narratives, the biggest war that has taken place in this country till date is Mahabharata. All attempts for peace were made before this Great War between Kauravas and Pandavas took place. Udyog Parva (i.e. the book of effort) of Mahabharata is written on that basis only. Yudhishthira and later Lord Krishna explored all the options possible with human intelligence, to prevent the war and arrange reconciliation between Pandavas and Kauravas. The war took place only after Kauravas did not agree to peace proposals and Duryodhana openly declared that he would not cede even an inch of land to Pandavas. This war was justified, as this was a war for righteousness.

Strength of Indian Consciousness

> *As per legendary narratives,the biggest war that has taken place in this country till date is Mahabharata. All attempts for peace were made before this Great War between Kauravas and Pandavas took place.*

Patience and restraint are the greatest strengths of Indian consciousness. We are not going to achieve anything by giving up these strengths. Renouncing patience and restraint would mean knowingly taking up the path of unrighteousness. Also, whose pride are we talking about to safeguard it, that of the nation or of some specific people? If we have to talk about safeguarding pride of some people, it would be a completely different matter. If we are talking about safeguarding the nation's pride or revival of a Hindu society or welfare of mankind, our path should be definitely entirely different. We would challenge, we would offer renunciation, and we would even sacrifice ourselves. However, this path of self-sacrifice would be the path of righteousness and the path of divinity. There should not be any system of self-sacrifice by following the path of unrighteousness. Nobody has attained God with the help of ritual killings and nobody has been able to awaken his spiritual consciousness by doing so. In Hindu philosophy, peace and protection exist alongside. On the one hand, amity and divine consciousness have been depicted in the form of universe. On the other hand, Lord Shankar has been depicted in the Tandava form and Goddess Kali in the form of a destroyer. The core consciousness of this country even reveres these forms. If required, the Indian intellect would not be afraid of even bloodshed. The nation would not hesitate to invoke Goddess Durga or Goddess Kali or even Lord Shankar if required for awakening of national consciousness. Before that, this would have to be confirmed if the right time for it has arrived. An appropriate time would come only after all openings for peace get closed. Even now, the paths of peace and talks are still available for finding a solution for the nation's problems, specifically social and cultural. Restraining ourselves from such talks or not coming forward for talks would be, in a sense, Adharma and doing anything that is against it is not going to be beneficial, at all.

□

13
Dharma and Rituals

The incident is quite old, but it is appropriate to mention it here as it is linked to the nation's soul and intellect. If conservatism, fanaticism and bigotry make even the President unhappy, mistreat him, insult him and get him entangled in the jugglery of rituals, the only thing that can be inferred out of the same is that Indian society has destroyed its creativity. Dharma is that which can become a perpetually flowing stream filled with the elixir of life. It is that which is full of spirit of common good and which cannot be chained by the shackles of rituals. Blind faith on rituals not only gives rise to hypocrisy but also makes a person perverse. This is what happened many years back, in 1988, at the sanctum sanctorum of the famous Nataraja temple in Chidambaram, Tamil Nadu. The then President Shri Venkataraman was not permitted to offer worship as he was wearing unacceptable clothes. He had to return dejected. When this incident took place, the Hindu priests could not criticise this hypocrisy influenced by rituals. Something similar exists even today. Hindu priests do not seem to be interested to free the Indian society from bigotry, hypocrisy and unnecessary rituals.

The interpretation that Indian consciousness has provided for Dharma does not stipulate any constraints of rituals and hypocrisy for Dharma. Hence, Hindu consciousness, as intelligence, is a supreme gift to the world. However, unfortunately, because of Hindus' own despondence, attachment and lethargy, Upanishad-centred Vedanta ideology is being led into captivity of hypocritical priests and devious religious leaders. An ideology that can the lead entire humanity to divine realisation of rationality is losing its strength just because it is today influenced by rituals and hypocrisy. This influence can be undone when we start giving rationality the maximum acceptance and gather strength to demolish irrational and illogical thinking. The country where even a President is unable to break the shackles of rituals and superstitions would have to make a long journey before it becomes the crown of world.

After observing the current scenario, it appears that we have erected plants and factories, constructed skyscrapers, built dams and have attained many other achievements on a material level. However, we are continuously going on getting dwarfed on a mental level and this mental degeneration or mental backwardness would ultimately give rise to problems only for us. Nobody can attain divine pleasure and divine happiness just by attaining material objects. Pleasure and happiness do not exist in objects. If pleasure and happiness were in objects, every common person would have attained the same by just getting that specific object. For instance, even wealthy people who have secured the best items for material happiness, call themselves happy, but are miserable because of their mentality. They are unhappy with their family, society and their relations with the society. That is the reason they are not able to have even a peaceful sleep. They need medicines even to sleep. Even a mild smile showing their happiness is absent on their faces. Is it really a life? On the other hand, those who live in poverty often have amazing sparkle of peace, happiness and self-satisfaction on their faces. The only reason for that is development of proper and well-balanced mind-set.

> *Pleasure and happiness do not exist in objects. If pleasure and happiness were in objects,every common person would have attained the same by just getting that specific object.*

Damaging Tolerance

Unbalanced, chaotic, shaken and a worried mentality, broken from the inside can never experience happiness. The mentality that is based entirely on self-interest cannot create divine love. The general mentality of Indian priests is based on self-interest. They have started doing a business of gods and goddesses. They are so much obsessed with arrogance that they have even renounced common decency. How would a priest or religious leader who does not know even common etiquette, do good for the society, the humanity and enable mankind to have a sight of divinity. The person who does not have a feeling of devotion and a feeling of respect towards his nation cannot have a feeling of devotion towards the world. How can the person who does not even know the alphabets, read the greatest scriptures and talk about it? And how can he understand it? It's not understandable how so many priests, worshippers and monks living in India and calling themselves devotees of God manage to progress in their lives. Perhaps, all this is happening because a common Indian does not want to confront these contradictory and hollow situations. He just tolerates them by ignoring them. Though tolerance is a heroic attribute, too much of tolerance gives rise to many troublesome problems in society. This hyper-tolerance of an average Hindu has given rise to such a class of hypocritical, heartless and even sometimes wicked people. They get themselves worshipped by presenting themselves at times, as God, as a divine soul and as an all capable, provider of happiness, vigour, fortune, dignity and heaven. There is a need now to be vigilant of this class.

> *Though tolerance is a heroic attribute,too much oftolerance gives rise to many troublesome problems in society. This hyper-tolerance ofan average Hindu has given rise to such a class of hypocritical,heartless.*

The truth is that spirituality is not an object of erudition. Spiritual thinking is not dependent on the blessings of priests and religious leaders. Any person is entirely free to indulge in best spiritual thinking. That is the reason we had Mahavira, Buddha, Kabir, Dadu and Ravidas in our country. Spiritual thinking is not related to dynasty. Excellent qualities and divine thinking cannot be inherited by a person as a natural course. They have to be acquired. If a person had swum across a vast turbulent river, it does not mean that his son also would have the capacity to swim across a turbulent river. The son would have to definitely learn swimming to be able to cross a turbulent river and also, he would have to be strong and resolute like his father. A person cannot receive such excellent qualities automatically by inheritance. But, in our country, priests and religious leaders hand out high qualities, sometime through talismans, sometime through ordination, sometime through chains and necklaces and sometime though the threads tied on wrists. It is difficult to think how long these 'traders' of Indian culture and philosophy and great spiritual ideology would continue to undermine our society and who would stop their misdeeds and how.

Business of Dharma

Hindus would have to now shape their lifestyle in accordance with their spiritual ideology. Until Hindus do that, the world would continue to laugh at them and call them hypocritical and devious only. What can we make out of the situation where the nation, Dharma and society that possesses a great ideology like Vedanta forget common things about morality and manners? The irony is that our average priests, religious teachers, monks, all appear to have forgotten the best qualities. Does this not mean that a part of Indian society is gripped by some or other grave malady? This malady has to be cured. Nobody can be healthy and happy by ignoring a malady. The malady would have to be cured; it does not matter which medicine system is used. Such maladies, which we call serious, do not get cured on its own without any medication. It's not clear when the Hindu society would medicate its disease and who would be the therapist, who the doctor and who would be that vaidya or hakim that would be capable of treating these patients. People are dispensing Dharma, people are trading in idols, people are cheating gullible public everywhere using chicanery, our places of pilgrimage and temples are being converted into centres of hypocrisy, rituals and superstitions and we are keeping quiet. Shrines and temples should be actually centres for divine consciousness. They should be actually sources of streams of supreme thoughts; but it's not happening like that. Our temples,

If a person had swum across a vast turbulent river,it does not mean that his son also would have the capacity to swim across a turbulent river. The son would have to definitely learn swimming to be able to cross a turbulent river.

mosques, churches and gurudwaras are falling in control of such persons who do not have any interest in real values of Dharma. These places have become centres for propagation of blemished consciousness. A proper introspection is required to rectify this situation. This introspection would have to be done with extreme patience. We would have to be constantly active with resolve, only then something would be possible. Only then something would be achieved and only then we would be able to offer something to humanity. For now, we are just getting drained out and what can a person who is getting drained out give to others?

This is Renounceable

This is an absolute truth that,in general terms,Hindu rituals are now badly afflicted by credibility gap. This credibility gaphas to be removed and we would have to create such rituals that do not promote any credibility.

Why can't our temples revive the nation? Why can't our temples assist in building a welfare society? Why can't those hypocrites and ritualists sitting in temples be removed? Rituals are not renounceable but if rituals are not in accordance with practicability and they are not able to adjust themselves to place, time and circumstances, they ultimately become shackles of conservatism. If rituals chain us with the shackles of customs, drain us, spoil our mental balance and create differences between our words and deeds, they are surely renounceable.

This is an absolute truth that, in general terms, Hindu rituals are now badly afflicted by credibility gap. This credibility gap has to be removed and we would have to create such rituals that do not promote any credibility gap. Rituals just work as a first step for attaining supreme spiritual consciousness. The mind gets tied to a natural discipline after performing some specific rituals continuously for some time, and with the help of a disciplined mind, we can uncover hidden mysteries of spiritual consciousness. The mind that is not disciplined cannot understand the minute and hidden mysteries of consciousness. This awakening of consciousness is possible only with a disciplined mind. There are many ways, as mentioned by our seers and sages, to attain this disciplined mind. A person is free to follow any of the procedures, but this choice should be made only after assessing his own capacity and circumstances to ensure success. Our average religious leaders are losing this capability and that is the reason that our temples, have turned from centres of spiritual consciousness, to centres of corruption. Here, dogs lick idols, rogue animals wander freely and defecate, all kinds of criminal acts take place, people are cheated, people are leered at and there is no immorality left that is not there. If this has to be rectified, we would have to make a resolve and revolt against those people who treat themselves as stakeholders of Dharma but refuse to break the shackles of conservatism.

□

14

How Would Communalism End Like This?

Would the misuse of constitution, judiciary, political system and fundamental rights continue in our country on the same lines as it has been happening for the last few years? Philosophers may say that when it's too dark in the night, one should assume that the sun is about to rise. There is no doubt that the country is currently going through a very dark phase. It's darkness, disappointment, frustration and resentment all around and there is no way in sight to save this country from this swirling vortex of agitated mind-set. Now this is very clear that when the mind is too agitated, it cannot make balanced decisions. And when our decisions start getting unbalanced, the truth becomes difficult to be saved and injustice gets predominant. This injustice may be aimed towards ourselves, opponents, society, the nation and humanity, but injustice is injustice after all. Injustice and justice can neither be complementary to each other not synonymous to each other. Both are opposite to each other.

Injustice cannot exist along with justice and where there is injustice, justice would not exist there. If we have to review the existence of justice at all levels, we need to find out if the right to justice is available to the living beings in general there. Just as a living creature has the right to live and to develop itself, it also has the right to justice under all circumstances. The philosophical ideologies of India are based on this very principle. Now it is a different matter that we are not able to safeguard it. We get confused, go astray - sometimes knowingly and sometimes unknowingly, and this disorientation is growing fast. If this disorientation were not so extensive, at least we would not be fighting even after almost fifty years of our independence to agree as to what actually is our Indian culture. There also would not have been any disagreements on what actually is communalism. Today, there is so much of difference of opinion in our country that a job that is treated as patriotic by a class of people does not come in the category of patriotism for others. Just for example, chanting 'Vande Mataram' was a symbol of patriotism before independence. Even for many years after independence, 'Vande Mataram' continued to be sung and the same continued to be treated as the core value of patriotism. Now after almost fifty years of independence, this idea is being floated in the Parliament that 'Vande Mataram' has nothing to do with patriotism. According to some of the members of Parliament, we would not be able to sing 'Vande Mataram' and not only that, even it was claimed that 'Vande Mataram' smacked of idol worship. They said that this was just a song written in the novel 'Anandmath' authored by Bankim Chand and this provoked communal hatred. Still more disturbing and regrettable is the fact that this kind of expression was supported by the ruling party - sometimes overtly and sometimes covertly. In the eyes of Congress Party, which has been in power most of the time after independence, the people who support this kind of opinion are patriots and those who oppose it are unpatriotic. Many such adjectives were used to refer to such people and the class of intellectuals in the society kept mum on the issue. Any disrespect to this chant of 'Vande Mataram' is disrespect to the nation, but our Prime Minister is not able to assert it in the Parliament.

According to some of the members of Parliament, we would not be able to sing 'Vande Mataram' and not only that, even it was claimed that 'Vande Mataram' smacked of idol worship. They said that this was just a song written in the novel.

In fact, the politics of today is developing a peculiar kind of mentality in the country. After all, where would such a politics that demolishes the self-respect of patriots lead the country? Would this politics now teach us to alienate ourselves from the truth? If politics is teaching us to alienate ourselves from truth, this also is certain that neither the ethics of our constitution nor its values nor its ideals nor its great traditions would remain safe. And then the country would be divided, it also would not be safe. There would be growth of mass destruction instead of mass development. Nobody appears to be concerned today to prevent the country from going on this doomed path. The only concern that exists is how to consolidate the vote bank.

Is this not an irony that while we do call upon people to fight against communalism, we also simultaneously differentiate people? That differentiation is also made in a way such that it gets covered under misunderstandings, suspicions and contradictions. Congress says, and rightly so, that all patriotic and secular people having faith in democracy should join together to fight those powers who want to take the country towards medieval era. This is very correct that people trying to push India towards medieval religious fanaticism are enemies of the nation; but who are doing all this?

Congress says, and rightly so, that all patriotic and secular people having faith in democracy should join together to fight those powers who want to take the country towards medieval era.

Definitely, the country cannot revert back to medieval religious hysteria. However, if it is being claimed that some Hindu organisations, especially Vishva Hindu Parishad, are making efforts to take the country back to that period, it is not based on facts. It's correct that the way a disputed structure was demolished at Ayodhya was unfortunate and that can also be called an act of vandalism. However, this has still not been established on the basis of facts that it was done by Vishva Hindu Parishad under some well-planned conspiracy. Even this has not been established by facts till now that this demolition of disputed structure was carried out by Bharatiya Janata Party. Involvement of the Rashtriya Swayamsevak Sangh in this demolition has also not been proven till now by any facts. Of course, it may be said that all these people were very happy on the demolition of that structure, though this was not appropriate. Demolition of a religious structure was an act that had resulted in contempt of Indian culture. Even if that structure were not demolished on 6 December, the temple would have got constructed on the same location. After all, crores of Hindus in the country assume to be Rama's birthplace and respect and bow their heads to. Rama's birthplace is a symbol of Hindus' faith and belief. The aggressor Babar had demolished the temple existing there to destroy this very faith and national pride. But most of the political parties in the country are knowingly ignoring this side of the truth. People indulging in this deliberate partisanship with demonic powers, partisanship with the enemies of the nation and partisanship with injustice would never be pardoned by the nation. This cannot be tolerated also. The temple would definitely be constructed on the same birthplace of Rama. When this happens is still not decided. However, any place of worship other than a temple cannot be constructed there. Whatever be the extent of weakness of our national consciousness, it is still not completely dead. It is still breathing and the number of breaths still available is sufficient to affirm that the nation would surely stand up once again to safeguard its self-respect. People who are real Indians have made themselves weak by getting melancholic; but they are now awakened. It's not possible to decoy them anymore. When a country or society awakens from a deep slumber, it remains dozy for some time but cannot go again to sleep soon. Now India is not going to sleep again very soon. It is its destiny now to arise, stand up, awaken, march ahead and provide leadership to the world again.

India that is to say Indian culture only would provide leadership to the world as Indian culture. Only Indian culture,has the capability to ful ly support Islam or any such religion or worshipsystem or sect or panth.

Ultimately, India that is to say Indian culture only would provide leadership to the world as Indian culture. Only Indian culture, has the capability to fully support Islam or any such religion or worship system or sect or panth, and love and accommodate it in its own domain. There is no other culture or religion or panth or ideology that is as liberal as Indian culture. There is no place in Islam for Indian culture, traditions, values and ideals. Even Christianity is not ready to respect the Indian worship system. This can be said in respect of Hindu culture or Indian culture. Every living being on this earth is a part of God in the eyes of every true Indian and hence is respectable and worth bowing head to. We Indians worship even trees; we not only worship human forms but also worship Sun and birds and animals; thus, even poisonous snakes are sacred for us as they are also a part of God's creations. Whatever is there in this Creation and has a bit of God is filled with divinity - that is our belief. Is there any such great ideology in any other philosophy, Dharma, religion or worship-system? But we have gone astray and hence do not talk sensibly.

Time and again, plans and policies are discussed for eliminating the poison of communalism. There is talk of seeking help from it sometime from leftists and sometime from others. Now, if this thinking is evaluated against the criteria of truth and values, nothing would be found more flimsy, disgusting and deplorable than it. How can we fight against communalism by getting separated in castes and sects? In fact, the education system of Macaulay and this culture brimming with Anglicism have given rise to an ideological misconception in the country. This has made the word 'Hindu' a symbol of communalism. The truth is otherwise, the word 'Hindu' is not a symbol of communalism and only a Hindu who is secular in real terms, is a true humanitarian and thinks of welfare for all. It is correct that the caste system has afflicted Hindu society, but this caste system is a social evil and has to be eliminated. There are many social evils in this country and we would have to stand against every social evil and fight and eliminate it. However, existence of some social evils in Hindu society does not mean there has to be some fundamental flaw in philosophical thinking of Hindus. There is no flaw in philosophical ideology. In fact, ideological class-hybridism is the biggest enemy of Indian culture today. This very ideological class-hybridism has not only made the entire country hollow and narrow-minded. It also has made it almost irrational, and all this has happened because of English oriented thinking and its evil effects.

Time and again,plans and policies are discussed for eliminating the poison of communalism. There is talk of seeking help from it sometime from leftists and sometime from others.

This is surprising that our leaders are not able to express clearly that the entire country should unitedly fight communalism. Our leaders divide the nation and make statements that backwards class, farmers and labour class should come forward to fight communalism. The question here is why the enlightened class should not come forward. After all, what wrong has been done by the teachers or the young generation or the lawyers that they should not come forward to fight communalism? Why should other intellectuals and other religious leaders of the country not unite to fight communalism? Why can't we say that all Hindus, Muslims, Sikhs, Christians and Parsis should come together to fight communalism? Not only that, even those people who do not believe in God should come forward. But, perhaps the politicians of this country do not want to indulge in such noble thinking, as it would not help them divide the country based on vote banks.

It's unfortunate that we are patronising this disaster that has already shaken the foundations of this country. Is this not true that the entire electoral calculations and election strategy of political parties of the country are dependent on equations of casteism and religious bigotry? When any strategy is formulated for election, the first thing that is considered is the caste of the candidate and the percentage of voters of the same caste in that constituency. Even within Hindus, proportions of schedules castes, backwards, Brahmins, Kshatriyas etc. are analysed and then distinctions are made among them. If the candidate is a Muslim, proportions of Shia and Sunni Muslims are analysed. This is all done to strengthen racial mentality and to satisfy political interests. Unfortunately, politicians are constantly following this very policy but neither Parliament nor judiciary nor bureaucracy has the courage to vehemently denounce it. This is that tragedy that is trying to forcibly stop the awakening of people's conscience. This is the irony that is encouraging communalism.

> *Why should other intel lectuals and other religious leaders ofthe country not unite to fight communalism? Why can't we say that al l Hindus,Muslims,Sikhs, Christians and Parsis should come together to fight communalism?*

Communalism is not linked only to religion, rather it is also related to caste, language and region. When we divide society between forwards and backwards, devise a caste system based on birth, ignore intelligence, link merit with caste or by-pass it to satisfy petty self-interests, we turn communalist. We would have to overcome all these weaknesses to safeguard our country from communalism. The idea that communalism can be eliminated by asking some castes and communities to fight against it is unfortunate and ludicrous.

Plans on paper cannot bring a change in ideology. We would have to move towards truth to change hearts. Only he who has tried to reach truth and has lived his life with full commitment to truth has actually attained truth. And the truth which is not truth in the real sense cannot find an effective solution to any problem. We have to become truth-explorers. We would have to definitely renounce the culture that does not express its full faith in national pride. As also the alien culture that disrespects Indian culture; only then we would be able to eliminate communalism from our country. Communalism is a racial word for Indian culture. There was no place for communalism in original Indian culture. It came into existence in our country only after we came in contact with alien culture. This is a malady that entered our body when we became dependent. We kept quiet when alien invaders oppressed, defeated and insulted Indian culture. If we need to know and understand the original form of Indian culture, we don't have to take help from leftists for it. They perhaps do not have any knowledge of India and Indian ideology and philosophy. And a blind cannot show the path to others. Hence, we should seek help from those who have knowledge and radiance and not from those who are sightless.

Plans on paper cannot bring a change in ideology. We would have to move towards truth to change hearts. Only he who has tried to reach truth and has lived his life with full commitment to truth has actually attained truth.

□

15

Constitution, Society and Religious Scriptures

Islam is an Arabic word and this word means peace, purity and commitment. Similarly, a Muslim is the one who dedicates his entire life to God. The core values of Islam are - 'Tawhid' i.e. oneness of God. This means that there is only one divinity pervading entire universe and no mischief should be done with others and one should not lie to others and treat others with feeling of brotherhood. But today, the process of divorce as prevalent in India is a stark example of how the people who claim to be followers of Islam are treating women unfairly.

Sometime back, the Lucknow bench of Allahabad High Court examined this process with the correct viewpoint of Islam, and more importantly, it tried to give respect to the supremacy of Indian constitution. However, conservative Muslim leaders raised serious objections and demanded that the lives of Indian citizens should be regulated only based on religious scriptures. Also, they were not concerned if that violated or corroborated the commitment that Indian constitution has made to all the citizens. Something similar is being said on the issue of the common citizen charter. And the irony is that all the politicians in the country are supporting such demands. The question here is - do politicians of our country offer allegiance to our constitution or to some 'religious scriptures'?

Progressive Muslims should express their concern over the way the process of divorce is being misused in Muslim society. This is not the path that is being followed by the Muslims in Egypt or Turkey or in such countries who claim to be fully Islamic and consider that their lifestyles to be fully based on Quran Sharif. India is not a country with state religion and hence, India would have to definitely accept the supremacy and universality of the constitution. Now it is a different matter that the current hard-line leaders in Muslim society want to create such an environment that may lead India to turn into a country with official state religion soon. A country with official state religion means a conservative country where entire politics, judiciary, administration, philosophy of life and way of life are regulated by some 'religious scriptures'. Are politicians like Sulaiman Sait trying to make India such a country only? If they really wish to make India such a country, let them say that openly. They cannot have the best of both worlds! It's also not possible that they retain the best of both the worlds intact and also enjoy the fruits. Although, if they want to make India a country with official state religion, that would never be possible. This is just contrary to Indian constitution and Indian philosophy and it is the responsibility of society today to oppose it.

Not sure when mankind would get civilised,well cultured and rational in real terms? Mankind has made a lot of progress,do not live in jungles any more,have become more generous, made discoveries and accomplished.

Not sure when mankind would get civilised, well cultured and rational in real terms? Mankind has made a lot of progress, do not live in jungles any more, have become more generous, made discoveries and accomplished conveniences to fulfill their needs. They have set many records for material prosperity and happiness, not only travel in space, but are also able to land on Moon and now they are even planning to go much beyond in space. It's also being claimed that time is not too far when the mankind would be able to uncover even the mystery of life and death; but, are these symbols of their real progress and civilisation? Has the soul of mankind changed, and if it has really changed, how much? Have they changed to the extent that it can be said without doubt that superstitions have no place in their lives? If a man believes in superstitions, desires to live a life dependent on conservatism and hypocrisy, wants to validate truth on the basis of books, wants to prove his intellectualism through quotes from them, especially 'religious scriptures' instead of rationality, reasoning, realisation and experience, can we still claim that he is a visionary of truth?

It's rather peculiar that the Indian society is divided into Hindus, Muslims, Sikhs and Christians sometimes in the guise of 'religious scriptures', language and region. The irony is that even in this situation, a man does not want to use his conscience to seek truth. He wants to fall back upon 'religious scriptures' as if truth is hidden only in those scriptures. If only the truth were actually hidden in those 'religious scriptures'! However, that is not the case, and this is the reason that the fights between truth and untruth and between justice and injustice are not getting resolved. Though there has been intellectual progress externally, the mind inside us is even today conservative, sceptical, irrational, superstitious, quarrelsome, selfish, autocratic and cowardly as ever. If a man were really courageous and free from fear, he would not have fallen back on 'religious scriptures' for his support and not have mollified his guilt with quotes from the 'spiritual heads'.

We have to fall back on reasoning and justice, get ourselves rid of sophism and review and analyse that specific book. Besides this, we would have to examine ourselves also with some self-sacrifice.

A visionary of truth would never confine himself to any specific book. Books do provide information, but to validate if there is truth in any information, we would have to use our conscience, undergo specific contemplation and cogitation. We have to fall back on reasoning and justice, get ourselves rid of sophism and review and analyse that specific book. Besides this, we would have to examine ourselves also with some self-sacrifice. Those who are visionaries of truth would never claim that truth has been definitely and ultimately uncovered or that wisdom and knowledge have reached their ultimate limits. When a brilliant person makes a new discovery with his labour, intelligence, knowledge, contemplation and cogitation, the previous knowledge becomes history and turns an important archaeological object. An archaeological object may certainly provide some information on the process of development of human civilisation, but any specific archaeological object cannot provide any clue as to future development of human civilisation. Truth can never be bound to any person or book. It can also never be bound by any period or region or country. In any case, truth cannot be discovered with the help of 'religious scriptures'.

If a 'religious scripture' makes a claim that the earth is flat, can it be accepted? Everybody knows that the earth is round and not flat; but if this is written in some 'religious scripture', it has to be ignored only. If it is written in some 'religious scripture' that God created the universe in six days and took rest for the seventh day and hence seventh day has to be treated as rest day, can this myth be treated as truth? This would be sheer foolishness. If it is written in some 'religious scripture' that God created Heaven with watercourses, dotted with date trees and there are beautiful girls available to those going to Heaven, can these fantasies be accepted today? The question here is not which 'religious scripture' contains what. The question here is why should those fabricated fantasies that are not valid on the criteria of truth, justice, rationality, realisation and experience should be given recognition today.

> *If it is written in some 'religious scripture' that God created the universe in six days and took rest for the seventh day and hence seventh day has to be treated as rest day, can this myth be treated as truth? This would be sheer foolishness.*

There are quite peculiar things written in 'religious scriptures'. Can this be accepted that a pillar cracked open and a person with his head of a lion and his body of a man came out of it and emancipated one of his devotees? Can we accept the stories that claim that a person had ten heads? We don't need to get into arguments as to why those fantasies were created; but truth cannot be uncovered with the help of those fantasies. Hence, the architects of Indian constitution did not take the help of 'religious scriptures' to define our nation's way of life. They took the assistance of reasoning, fairness and rationality and used their realisation and experience to set such criteria. Those that stipulated provision of justice, freedom and equality to all citizens and made sure that the dignity of every person was safeguarded. When a reference was made to dignity of a person, no distinction was made between a man and a woman. Hence, whether it is related to divorce or any other matter, men and women have the same rights, and they surely deserve equal rights. What constitutes justice cannot be defined based on religious scriptures. Seeking justice is now an established and universal principle and it should be examined only on the basis of established and universal principles if justice is being delivered or not.

The way the controversy was raised in respect of divorce and uniform civil code indicates how weak, superstitious and conservative we Indians are mentally. It does not matter whether Justice Tilhari of Lucknow bench of Allahabad High Court was right or wrong on the issue of divorce, but the real point is whether he really did any injustice to Indian women. If Justice Tilhari did not do any injustice and his decision was rational, reasonable, practical and pragmatic, why is there a hue and cry? If he was going to enhance the dignity of mankind, eliminate exploitation and genuine on the criterion of equality, why there is so much opposition? Is the right to justice available only to men and not women? Are we going to fall back on 'religious scriptures' to decide whether exploitation is taking place or not? And if yes, how long we should be doing that? The idea that we should attempt to banish superstitions and conservatism by winning people's hearts is sheer foolishness. Here, it must be understood once for all that it is never possible to please everybody and also it is not possible to win heart of every person. A revolutionary or an architect of an era does not care what people say or what people want, rather he only thinks of what truth is, what is rational and what history has taught him. If only we Indians could understand the difference between mobocracy and democracy! Mobocracy can never become democracy and likewise. Democracy can exist only where rationality and dissension are respected, where there is place for equality, justice and brotherhood instead of exploitation and conservatism. If exploitation and injustice are taking place in the guise of 'religious scriptures' and we do not come

The way the controversy was raised in respect of divorce and uniform civil code indicates how weak,superstitious and conservative we Indians are mental ly.

forward to eliminate it, it would be appalling. Calling that system a democracy i.e. rule by people, would be insult to the word 'people'. In a democracy, the word 'people' refers to the persons who have faith in the principles of rationality, brotherhood and tolerance. Every such person is undemocratic who is not ready to provide others the same rights that he wants for himself.

Men and women have been provided the same rights under the Indian constitution. Nowhere is it mentioned that any specific right would be meant only for women or any other right only for men. When men and women have equal rights, why should there be discrimination in their marital matters? Why are those people who always used to cry for social justice silent today? Where are those so-called champions of social justice and those who keep on making various denouncements against our Indian culture? Why don't they want to come forward and declare that men and women have got same rights in this country irrespective of whether they are Hindu or Muslim or follower of any other religion? Is the Indian constitution going to create a framework of social rights separately for people of different religions? Definitely this has been a great mistake of architects of Indian constitution that they omitted to clearly formulate that all citizens of this country would have to follow a common civil code. It's unfortunate that whenever nation gets an opportunity for an ideological revolution, these hypocritical politicians otherwise raising voices for social justice go into hiding like rats. They use their slogans for social justice only for creating their vote banks. No doubt, their slogans for social justice can generate hatred and divisions in the society and can never create an environment for social justice in real terms. The silence of these sloganeers of social justice at the time of ideological revolution proves them to be escapist politicians only, who cannot provide social justice to society. Otherwise also, how can those politicians who are not ready to even safeguard the dignity of women take a partisan stand for social justice?

Men and women have been provided the same rights under the Indian constitution. Nowhere is it mentioned that any specific right would be meant only for women or any other right only for men.

If a 'religious scripture' or any part of it makes us weak, favours injustice, teaches us exploitation, distrust, deceit and dishonesty, we need to keep away. We should keep away from its parts too, that support injustice, irrespective of the religion that scripture belongs to. We should review the scriptures to explore what is rational and what is fallacy, harmful to mankind. If man gives up his conscience and rationality, he would not be able to progress. Knowledge and conscience are infinite and no one book can claim to contain entire knowledge and conscience. Truth can never be unveiled in an ultimate sense. It is a continuous process of discovery of that knowledge and conscience that helps a person to develop his creative energy and consciousness for common good. Discovery of truth is an awakening. A person pursuing truth can never be retrogressive meaning that such a person cannot be a proponent of narrow-mindedness, conservatism, superstitions and violence. Injustice is also a kind of violence. It's unfair to treat oneself as superior and others as fallen. This injustice has to be opposed and if India does not come forward to oppose this injustice, we would be ultimately compelled to accept that India is still in intellectual and psychological bondage. If 'religious scriptures' are making us slaves intellectually, we would have to unshackle this bondage and free every person of this country from slavery, brutality and exploitation which has been brought about by them.

If a 'religious scripture' or any part of it makes us weak, favours injustice, teaches us exploitation, distrust, deceit and dishonesty, we need to keep away.

This is a commitment of all the citizens of India that 'each and every person would be entitled to social, economic and political justice'. If women of this country are not getting social justice, who is responsible? If judiciary is not discharging its responsibility, why should there not be any criticism? The way Justice Tilhari was criticised on the issue of divorce or the Supreme Court was criticised on the issue of common civil code is against the Constitution and disgraceful for the judiciary. It is a different issue that judiciary does not have the courage to come forward to punish those disrespecting our constitution in respect of 'religious scriptures' and rights of women. The way social and political pressures are being exerted on judiciary is extremely unfortunate. This must be combated while there is still time, to secure social & economic justice and honour, and safeguard the dignity of every person, as mentioned in the Constitution.

□

16

Adharma in the name of Dharma

It's difficult to make out when a solution would be found for this incessant degeneration of Indian society being caused by the word 'Dharma' or in the name of 'Dharma'. This very degeneration was the cause of partition of the country. Still, no improvement could be accomplished in this degeneration even after independence and Indian society, though religious, has kept on falling apart. Even if we agree that there is a limit of disintegration, it now appears that this disintegration is going on growing like Surasa's mouth! The irony is that nobody is able to make out when and how this disintegration would end. After all, it is the result of this degeneration that while some years ago we heard slogans like 'we would not celebrate Republic Day and we would unfurl 'Black flags'. And today, we are coming across comments suggesting that the country would be converted into a Hindu nation and Indian Constitution would be amended. Before independence, we were indulging in killings and bloodsheds in the name of 'Dharma' and now after independence we are doing it with greater intensity. No such riots had taken place in this country after independence as those that took place recently in Mumbai, Surat and Ahmedabad. It appeared during these riots that devilishness was taking over humans in the name of 'Dharma'. This is also a form of degeneration that anybody is ready to preach to others on 'Dharma' without thinking, understanding or contemplating. After all, what is this 'Dharma'? Somebody says that 'Dharma' means only telling beads, offering prayers to gods and goddesses and worshipping idols. Somebody else claims that offering sacrifices is 'Dharma'. 'Dharma' has also been linked to costumes, food habits and education. To sum up, there are as many views of 'Dharma' as there are mouths. Hence, when a person is not able to or does not want to understand the point made by another person, it gives rise to clashes and violence and spreads hatred and hostility. All this happens in the name of 'Dharma'. This should have stopped in independent India, but that did not happen.

The Constitution of India does not support this degeneration taking place in the name of 'Dharma' but it is also unable to stop it. Perhaps the biggest reason for it is that the word 'Dharma' has become a part of Indian politics and vote banks are being created using it. Opinions of voters are being influenced and attempts are being made to protect petty political interests. In this regard, a point of concern is that the politician who talks of 'Dharma' presents his views in such a way as if he himself has encountered truth. Today, most of the politicians are using their arbitrary interpretations of 'Dharma' to poison the society in a way that would ultimately damage the society badly. Unfortunately, this hypocrisy in the name of 'Dharma' is prevalent even in religious gurus and can be observed even in the Parliament. This is in any case clearly visible outside the Parliament. In short, perhaps no aspect of Indian life would be there that is not impacted by these arbitrary interpretations of 'Dharma'. And now these interpretations have grown to such an extent that it appears as if there is no end to it.

The Constitution of India does not support this degeneration taking place in the name of 'Dharma' but it is also unable to stopit. Perhaps the biggest reason for it is that the word 'Dharma' has become a part of Indian politics and vote banks.

The truth is that 'Dharma' is related to actual personal life meaning that every person has the right to choose his 'Dharma'. If every person has the right to choose his 'Dharma', there would be as many interpretations of 'Dharma' as the number of persons. It is here assumed to mean only the worship system. The fact, however, is that 'Dharma' should have no relation with the worship system, as Dharma is that element which defines the existence of an object, e.g. burning is the Dharma of fire. However, the word 'Dharma' is generally interpreted in a limited sense. These limited interpretations are useful neither for attainment of knowledge nor for seeking that realisation of knowledge, essential for pursuing the path of truth. The people who claim that they would fight against the insanity of 'Dharma' are being hypocritical as 'Dharma' is neither insane nor a reason for anybody going so. 'Dharma', in fact, is capable of infusing divinity in a person. It provides those procedures that may help a person overcome all his depravities. 'Dharma' just validates that this body in bones and flesh is really a human, but even understanding this philosophical interpretation does not help in its attainment. Whatever is happening today in the name of 'Dharma' is because we do not have a clear definition of what and how, regarding its form and usage. This was a mistake on the part of architects of the Constitution of India that they did not attempt to define the words 'Dharma' and 'secular'. Had they made such an attempt and had they committed any mistake, it could have been deliberated over later for correction. However, when there has not been any attempt at all, where is the question of any mistake and correction? Unfortunately, even today, neither our Parliament nor our judiciary appears to be inclined to make any such attempt. Not only that, even the so-called 'Dharma sansad' is also not ready to provide a clear and unambiguous definition of 'Dharma'. Of course, slogans like 'Victory for Dharma', 'Death to Adharma, 'Let there be goodwill among humans' and 'Welfare for the world' are raised today on different platforms. However, even the people who raise them are not aware what their slogan 'Victory for Dharma' actually means and what Adharma actually is. People who raise such slogans generally assume that applying sandalwood or reading the Ramayana or reading the Gita is 'Dharma'. This also means that believing in a particular worship system and performing rituals is Dharma and people who do not make any specific worship system and rituals part of their life don't follow it. If 'Dharma' is cast into such a narrow-minded form, how can there be goodwill all around and how can there be welfare for the world? If some people want that all others follow a specific worship system only, this would not help spread goodwill. If anybody does not believe in a particular worship system, it would not be 'Dharma' to oppose and disbelieve him. This would be a path of narrow-

If some people want that all others follow a specific worshipsystem only, this would not help spread goodwill. If anybody does not believe in a particular worship system, it would not be 'Dharma' to oppose and disbelieve him.

mindedness. The irony is that today, such kind of narrow-mindedness is growing in this country and that is the reason there is unease and unrest all around.

Sometime back, erstwhile Chief Minister Mulayam Singh Yadav declared that he would fight with full force against the idiosyncrasies of 'Dharma'. His statement looks very appropriate on shallow level, but what is the reality? The reality is that Mulayam Singh Yadav is attempting to restart his vote bank politics to ensure that backward classes and scheduled castes come together. The question here is, why only these groups should come together? In fact, this has been an attempt by Mulayam Singh Yadav to wreck the popularity that Bharatiya Janata Party has secured on account of the movement for Rama's birthplace. Mulayam Singh treats all that has been done or being done by Bharatiya Janata Party for the construction of Rama's temple as idiosyncrasies of 'Dharma'. In this context, Lal Krishna Advani is making a statement that he is using 'Dharma' to awaken the country and not for his political interests. In short, whatever Advani is saying is an idiosyncracy for Mulayam Singh, whereas, for Advani, it is sacred and revolutionary, without which India may not be able to safeguard its existence. Definitely, both cannot be correct; one of the two is correct and the other is telling a lie. If both of them are telling a bit of lie, some effort must be made to discover the truth. It is worth considering that 'Dharma' has never been constrained by definitions in our country, instead, emphasis has been placed on attaining realisation by linking it with karma. In other words, embrace all the best principles in your life and attain realisation. Today, we are just trying to imprison 'Dharma' within the limits of definitions only. Though, in view of the current circumstances, it would be proper to define 'Dharma' in such a way that this word is not misused. One of the definitions of 'Dharma' could be that all creatures come within its purview and the entire universe is based on it only. In other words, whatever is righteous, whatever is reasonable and whatever can make

Mulayam Singh treats all that has been done or being done by Bharatiya Janata Party for the construction of Rama's temple as idiosyncrasies of 'Dharma'.

a person a citizen of the highest order is 'Dharma'. All those works that would help society progress and result in the welfare of society are also 'Dharma'. However, presenting a definite interpretation of 'Dharma' being difficult today due to the prevalent enmities, most of the politicians are busy, serving their petty political interests through it.

It's a tragedy for India that vote politics has made it extremely craven psychologically. Nobody is able to muster the courage to counter the misconceptions, especially of 'Dharma', prevalent in the country. It was expected that at least the Parliament would gather that strength. However, the Parliament is all the more proving to be impotent. In other words, the kind of politics, currently in vogue at the level of Parliament is degrading the country, all the more. Everybody agrees that this degradation needs to be stopped, but nobody is ready to discuss rationally, the ways to stop it. Man has almost renounced his rationality by constraining 'Dharma' to books and preaching, and linking it to temples, mosques, gurudwaras and churches, paying a heavy price for it. The truth is that 'Dharma' is not related to places of worship. Places of worship should be given importance and used only to discipline our minds and maintain peace. Otherwise also, these institutions were possibly created for this very purpose only. Another purpose that seems probable might be to create such a zone where people with similar ideologies could sit together, try to discover and attain the happiness that they always longed for. These places of worship provide just one of the ways that are available to man for attaining the joy and happiness that he always desires. Presently, this has also got linked to politics, especially vote bank politics and politics for grabbing and sticking to power. The situation has gone worse and instead of attaining peace and happiness, man is getting afflicted by enmity and unrest and becoming hostile to each other.

It's a tragedy for India that vote politics has made it extremely craven psychologically. Nobody is able to muster the courage to counter the misconceptions, especially of 'Dharma', prevalent in the country.

Those who know the core values of 'Dharma' and really understand it can neither be conservative nor form their own community. They cannot start their own sect nor harbour the feeling of defeating another group by creating their own group. All these things only are however happening today in the name of 'Dharma' and are being done by the people who want to carry on with their hypocrisy in the guise of 'Dharma'. This hypocrisy gets reflected sometime in the form of Islamic state, sometime in the form of Christian state and sometime in the form of Hindu state. The question here is what India wants and why can't India remain just as India? Does India need any special adjective to remain as India? What is this Hindu India or Muslim India? Will there be no place for Muslims or followers of other worship systems in Hindu India? If Hindu India means imposing a ban on the minds of people or a ban on their thinking power, will that Hindu India be India of our dreams? In fact, the best thing would be to leave India as India only.

Those who know the core values of 'Dharma' and really understand it can neither be conservative nor form their own community. They cannot start their own sect nor harbour the feeling of defeating another group by creating their own.

Incidentally, the word 'Hindu' is not a Sanskrit word. This word did not originate in India. It is a different matter that by the passage of time, this word that came from Arabia has changed its meaning and intention. The word 'Hindu' started to refer to people believing in some specific worship system. Indian culture that is also called Hindu culture does not have anything to do with narrow-mindedness. No narrow-minded or conservative person can be a Hindu; only a person with highly liberal and generous mentality can be a real Hindu. And the person who has a highly liberal and generous mentality does not need adjectives; instead he resides in the consciousness of the whole. The whole is his 'Dharma'. Manifestation of the whole only is his duty. Establishment of the feeling of the whole is his resolve. The main reason for degeneration of the Indian society is the fact that we have renounced this feeling of the whole. It is not clear how and when we are going to attain our basic elements and appreciate them again. However, it would be better to at least stop using the word 'Dharma' in the sense of narrow-mindedness until we realise and understand the essence of the whole.

□

17

Dharma and Atheism

There is no such person who likes unrest. Even a person looking quite disturbed and furious externally is ignorantly following the path of disturbance and violence for actually seeking peace. This search for peace is the ultimate aim of life. Nobody wants misery in his life. Every person wants to be away from unrest and discord. It is the goal of a man to seek pleasure and happiness. This thirst for attaining pleasure and happiness, in whatever way possible, is found everywhere. The mystery of self-interest is hidden in this very search for pleasure and happiness. The very purpose of self-interest is to attain pleasure and happiness for self. The entire buzz around and all the struggles in life are centred on the fulfillment of one desire, how to make the entire consciousness and world pleasant and blissful for self. Nobody, irrespective of whether he is a theist or an atheist, wants to even have a glimpse of grief. The very thought of grief makes a person uneasy. Every person today has the desire to make this world pleasant for himself, even if that means making the world miserable for others. All the trading taking place, the principles being sold and purchased and the ideologies being propagated as 'Dharma' are meant to make this world pleasant, prosperous, blissful and well-cultured. Likewise, those who claim not to follow any Dharma and believe in any related organisation or principle, also maintain that their goal is to make this world pleasant, prosperous and more civilised. In this limited sense, there is no difference between the philosophy of life of a theist and that of an atheist. But still, neither an atheist is ready for coexistence with a theist nor is a theist ready for coexistence and cohabitation with an atheist. Both appear to be fanatic and sometimes violent opponents to each other. Neither of the two are ready to nourish the other. Each of the two mocks the other and calls him ignorant and foolish. According to an atheist, a theist lives his life just under superstitions and hypocrisy, and a theist considers an atheist completely ignorant and foolish. He believes that an atheist can never enjoy pleasure and happiness. A theist confidently believes that atheists would continue to always face abject misery, encounter varied agonies and there would not be no end to their hardships.

This conflict between theists and atheists is possibly eternal, not a recent phenomenon. A theist says - maintain devotion, have faith, you would be rewarded; an atheist says - first reason, contemplate, examine and then look for happiness in this visible world. There is no place for faith in the life of an atheist and he does not recognise words like devotion and worship. His life is meant for his own happiness. Anybody or anything other than the self is extraneous and a person would have to first of all think of his own happiness and prosperity, this is the primary thinking of an atheist. When this thinking of the 'self' gets importance of its supremacy at the level of class or society, with common culture, it takes the form of a nation on further progress. When that 'self' enters politics, it takes the form of power. The thinking of an atheist is not able to go beyond this. An atheist believes that all achievements till date is the result of mankind's hard labour and intelligence. Hence, he would uncover all the mysteries of Nature with his strength, intelligence and wisdom and would use them for the benefit of his 'self'. 'Self' here refers to 'I'. The word 'self' may include even community and organisation, but the word 'I' is purely personal. This 'self' is in a sense an extension of 'I' and the person who thinks of 'self' and gives it importance and preference, is actually 'I' centred. Atheism is related to 'I' centred consciousness only. For an atheist, the existence of 'I' only is supreme and eternal and that only is the reason for happiness and pleasure and that only enjoys them.

Anybody or anything other than the self is extraneous and a person would have to first of all think of his own happiness and prosperity, this is the primary thinking of an atheist.

An atheist denies any inspirational and effective existence of anything else other than himself. In a sense, the personality of an atheist is the 'outrageous extreme' of his own self-confidence. Hence, he does not accept existence of any such being that is too humane. For an atheist, only those things that can be known and understood at a person's level and at the level of his intelligence and senses are truth. Anything that cannot be understood with the help of intelligence and senses and cannot be directly experienced in any way is neither true nor in existence. The reason an atheist denies the existence of Dharma is that it talks of entering into consciousness of the whole by going beyond the scope of mind, senses and intelligence. As Dharma in its eternal form neither wants to get constrained by principles nor comes within the perimeter of experience, it appears to be imaginary and hypocritical to an atheist.

Even the philosophy of an atheist has a history. It's not that atheism did not get any support in India where all-dimensional form of Dharma was ideated, but as per Indian philosophy, atheism means getting only naturalistic. An atheist does not connect himself with God, soul, Paramatma, spirituality or any such concepts that are related to supreme human. He even does not believe the idea of heaven and hell. In short, an atheist is more rational. His entire belief, faith and confidence are devoted to intelligence and that also temporal intelligence only. This is the biggest weakness of an atheist. He refuses to know and understand the limits of intelligence and wants to encompass everything within the limits of intelligence only. He is not able to understand that even intelligence is just an instrument for man's use and the level of intelligence is below the level of a man and not above. This is correct that whatever a man can find out and understand in his normal life is achieved with the help of his intelligence only; but how can any person claim that there is no life and no existence at all beyond intelligence? Anybody may understand that intelligence is dependent on senses for

Even the philosophy of an atheist has a history. It's not that atheism did not get any support in India where al l-dimensional form of Dharma was ideated, but as per Indian philosophy, atheism means getting only naturalistic.

its actions and reactions and man has got only five sense organs. If man had more number of senses, they would have had greater impact on the decisions made by intelligence. Hence, this claim that whatever is understood by intelligence is ultimate truth is entirely baseless. How can anybody know the system that exists beyond intelligence with the help of intelligence? How can anybody reach the domain with the help of intelligence where there is no momentum for intelligence? Dharma goes beyond senses in its pure spiritual form; hence the mysteries of Dharma cannot be uncovered only with the help of power or shrewdness of intelligence. Atheists have made their entire thinking very narrow and temporal by making this, intelligence and sense oriented. Dharma, on the other hand, particularly in its form of supreme consciousness, is not only liberal but also infinite and timeless. Intelligence is born out of Dharma and not the other way round. However, in this context, Dharma does not refer to any such idea that is communal and constrained by scriptures and books and principles or that is just a bundle of moral values and ethics.

> *Dharma goes beyond senses in its pure spiritual form; hence the mysteries of Dharma cannot be uncovered only with the helpof power or shrewdness of intel ligence. Atheists have made their entire thinking very narrow.*

Though an atheist may deny the existence of Dharma, his consciousness keeps on roaming always within the purview of Dharma only. The atheist may or may not call Dharma by name, he may not have any faith in Dharma, but still his mind is always impatient to uncover all eternal mysteries. Those, which are the objects for contemplation by a theist. 'Who am I?', 'Where have I come from?', 'What is my end?', 'What is birth?', 'What is death?', 'Why is there misery?', 'What is misery?', 'Is there any freedom from misery?', 'Is there any existence of the consciousness of eternal bliss?', 'Is it possible to enter the state of that bliss?', 'Can peace be attained?' - there are many questions like these that an atheist is not able to answer reasonably. It is the arrogance of an atheist that prevents him from intense discovery of the supreme spirit. An atheist's thinking is so extroverted that it has renounced even the idea of getting introverted. However, only the person who is ready to introspect and is committed for a complete surrender of his soul and abandonment of self can attain Dharma. Only he who has faith on the whole instead of individual can understand the truth of righteousness. An atheist is in any case completely egoistic and individualistic. He refuses to even accept the existence of consciousness of the whole or totality. But his denial cannot in any case make the consciousness of the whole disappear. All his works, entire philosophy, all thinking lie within the perimeters of the whole. There is no way that an atheist may separate himself in the real sense from consciousness of the whole. The whole means 'total existence' and there is no way at all to get separated from this 'total'. Whether an atheist wants it or not, he cannot violate the existence of the whole, the Param Chaitanya. Howsoever, an atheist may refuse to accept indescribable existence of 'Anandamaya kosha' and Param Chaitanya, how he would deny the realisation that there is some eternal element that is the basis of his self and his entire existence. How would an atheist deny that when he utters the words 'I slept quite well today' after getting up from a sound sleep, there must be some element that would have experienced that sound sleep? If the atheist becomes conscious of that element, realised under sound sleep and deep trance, that it was under these very elements, he would enter the perimeters of spiritual consciousness. That element which always remains awake and conscious must be certainly separate from the body. It neither resizes as per body nor maintains any direct identification with body, but just resides in the body and uses it. However, the atheist is neither awake to these interpretations nor accepts them, as they are not related to normal life and intelligibility of senses.

> *It is the arrogance of an atheist that prevents him from intense discovery of the supreme spirit. An atheist's thinking is so extroverted that it has renounced even the idea of getting introverted.*

The atheist does not believe in eternality and timelessness or universality of life element. He feels that presence of the life element in the body or the presence of the life element in Nature is just a chemical or accidental coincidence. This means that when some elements of the

Nature combine together at a place or body or point for some reason or coincidence, it results in the creation of a life element. As per an atheist, the life element gets created when favourable conditions exist, hence the creation of the life element is possible even in a laboratory if favourable conditions could be created there. The scientific research that is currently going on in respect of this life element matches to a great extent with this thinking, and are certain to get uncovered sooner or later. The atheist has no belief in the theory that this life element has some eternal Dharma. The atheist does not connect himself with the feeling or concept of the life element that is referred to as supreme energy or Param Chaitanya or Paramatma in spiritual language. However, after all those scientific discoveries, the atheist today is at least ready to accept that the world is nothing but manifestation of energy only. If we go on disintegrating anything that is visible in this world and anything that can be felt, we would get energy only in the end. On this very basis, science has announced that unit of every matter is energy only and energy neither has any specific form nor can be constrained with the limits of place or time. This energy is infinite, universal and eternal. After this declaration by science, the present atheist thinking also has accepted this eternal existence of energy. This very belief of an atheist is 'Param Chaitanya' for theists and they address this only as the basis of this universe i.e. Paramatma. The theist claims that the form of this Param Chaitanya or Paramatma cannot be perceived and the ultimate finding of science also states that the source and form of energy cannot be perceived.

The scientific research that is currently going on in respect of this life element matches to a great extent with this thinking, and are certain to get uncovered sooner or later. The atheist has no belief in the theory that this life element has some eternal Dharma.

The main reason for the fierce opposition by atheist thinking against existence of 'Dharma' and 'Paramatma' is the perversity of theists claiming Paramatma to be a super human. This also includes the idea of the creator of this world residing far away in seventh heaven, providing happiness and prosperity when pleased, and inflicting tortures, miseries and sufferings, when displeased. Theists propagated this kind of deism or providence. They even prescribed different kinds of procedures to please 'Paramatma' or 'God' and created sects and organisations to please them. Shops started functioning in the name of 'Paramatma' and 'God' on that very basis. The main objection of atheists would have been against this business or deism or priestism. Priestism even believes that Paramatma likes sycophancy and he can also be cruel and a tormentor. Oppression, exploitation, bloodshed and even war were justified to provide recognition to the existence of Paramatma. When baseless concepts started growing, they were opposed and atheism started getting acceptance. Such things have happened on this earth in almost all eras and almost all countries have gone through periods of oppression in the name of Dharma and Paramatma. Atheists could not really understand this fact that 'Paramatma', used for the purpose of exploitation was actually created by priestism for its own self-interest based on its own imaginations. Just for the purpose of serving petty self-interests, the name of 'Paramatma' was used to create many fantasies and develop several stories that had nothing to do with 'Supreme Being'. Paramatma was made emperor in some fantasies whereas in others, he was depicted as the propagator of principles, social regulations and material regulations. Some linked him to Nature's powers while others linked him to superstitions and hypocrisy and heaven and hell. Thus, such 'imaginary Paramatma' and irrational 'Dharma' were sure to get opposed. Hypocrisy and superstition can never stand for long. It's a natural phenomenon for such things to get opposing voices in society. Those who opposed also gave a name to themselves and called themselves agnostic and those very people were later called atheists.

The main objection of atheists would have been against this business or deism or priestism. Priestism even believes that Paramatma likes sycophancy and he can also be cruel and a tormentor.

The questions here are, 'Are these atheists irrational?', 'Why do they accept mental restlessness?', 'Do they really want to keep themselves aloof from the discovery of bliss or complete truth?' Surely it is not so. It is correct that materialism is the greatest power of an atheist's consciousness but even materialism ultimately wants to attain peace and bliss. The biggest strength of materialism is science. It is the purpose of science to create consistently more resources for comfort, happiness and prosperity of mankind. Science can never be based on superstition or hypocrisy. It is based on rationality and in the same way, atheism also uses rationality as its own base. However, there is a lot of difference between rationality of an atheist and that of science. The rationality of science is not based on stubbornness; it always remains alive to new thoughts and does not refuse to accept or examine them. On the other hand, the rationality of the atheist shuts its eyes towards new thoughts; an atheist is filled with stubbornness and perversity, whereas science is quite far from perversity.

It's very less likely that the current situation with atheism flourishing unabated would continue for long. Humanity is being stricken by perversity, stubbornness and too much materialism of atheism.

It's very less likely that the current situation with atheism flourishing unabated would continue for long. Humanity is being stricken by perversity, stubbornness and too much materialism of atheism. At the same time, the persons who are really rational can never renounce rationality. 'Dharma' has no conflict with rationality; rather Dharma arouses us towards Param Chaitanya and towards ourselves. This awakening of inner self is the first step of Dharma. This very awakening of rationality and inner self would ultimately destroy the existence of atheism. Conscious perception of truth can be achieved only with rationality and this very rationality is the soul of Dharma.

□

18

May Our Shankaracharyas Move Further Ahead

Adi Shankara had unfolded and understood the secrets of Dharma by entering into divine consciousness. Had the disciples of Adi Shankara shaped themselves as per that consciousness, Indian society would not have undergone the kind of degradation that exists today. The most respected Adi Shankara perceived only one Virat Chaitanya everywhere and this very non-dual perception that 'the same form of divinity exists in everything and any feeling of dualism is because of ignorance' became the core value of his life. 'The feeling of dualism is born out of self-amnesia and Paramatma resides in everybody' - had this great philosophy been adopted in Indian public life, our nation would have been providing leadership in every field to this world today. But this could not happen.

It's not that Adi Shankara did not do enough for publicising and propagating his philosophy of non-duality. He went to all corners of the country. He travelled in all directions, demolished hypocrisy and superstitions and established four Mathas, at Sringeri, Dvaraka, Puri and Badrika. It is believed that after this, Adi Shankara settled for life at Kancheepuram and conducted discourses to provide guidance for common good. It's not clear why this feeling of common good did not get adopted in the general public life of India. Even after the death of Adi Shankara, seers and great scholars continued to visit the Mathas established by him, and the Mathas are still well established. However, these Mathas could not rekindle any such flame of enlightenment that would have eliminated the gruesome form of animosity, discrimination and narrow-mindedness that exists all around our country. These Mathas also did not attempt to organise the public of our country to fight against the cultural invasion of the West and to arouse their national self-esteem. Presently, superstition and blind faith are given more importance in all the discussions related to Dharma. The Mathas do not organise any meaningful discussions on issues like the philosophy of life. Issues required for Indian society for welfare and development of nation and humanity or ways and means needed for eradication of evils of Indian society.

Adi Shankara never considered the word 'Dharma' as communal. He actually provided a very comprehensive interpretation of the word 'Dharma'. He perceived Dharma as a form of Paramatma. He never believed that Dharma could be attained only through rituals. However, his disciples considered rituals as everything. Today, none of the Mathas is doing anything for transformation of the inner self. Many shops are being run today in the name of Adi Shankara. Adi Shankara had established only four Mathas, but nobody knows how many other Mathas have been established today with the 'patronage' and 'favour' from politicians and because of narrow-mindedness of saffron-clad people. Today, anyone and everyone is trying to proclaim himself as Shankaracharya and it appears there is a flood of Shankaracharyas in the country. If these shops were not established, the ideas of Adi Shankara would have been able to do good to the country; but who is worried about the welfare of country today? Nobody is at all talking today about raising voices against the situation of anarchy. The way hypocrisy and superstition are growing in this country indicates that the future of India is still dark. If only the Shankaracharyas of today could have done something to eradicate this hypocrisy and superstition! Definitely, it is the duty of the people occupying seats of Shankaracharyas to come forward for eradication of evils and maladies of our society. At least, untouchability, hypocrisy, superstitions and casteism existing

Adi Shankara had established only four Mathas, but nobody knows how many other Mathas have been established today with the 'patronage' and 'favour' from politicians.

in Indian society should definitely stop. Why should any person in the society be treated as dalit? In our Vedic literature, every human being has been addressed as 'अमृतस्य पुत्रा:' (*'amritasya putra'*) meaning every male and female is a form of God only. But current Indian consciousness is not able to accept this notion as part of their life and that is the reason narrow-mindedness, discord, superstition and frustration are spreading all around in our society. It appears that as the number of saffron-clad people is increasing in temples and Mathas of the country, the problems in our society are also increasing. Our current Shankaracharyas are not able to take any concrete steps for the remedy of these problems. They have more faith on conservatism in the name of tradition. Certainly it is an insult to the intellectual strength of India to give importance to superstition over rationality. It is of course expected from our current Shankaracharyas to have commitment and resolve to adore and honour knowledge and to eradicate ignorance. Residing in spiritual consciousness or divine consciousness does not mean overlooking the evils and maladies of society and problems of the country. This would not be appropriate. It is unfortunate to note that some of our Shankaracharyas have started to discriminate between man and woman and are declaring that women do not have right to study Vedic literature. What kind of point of view is this? This is just a blatant injustice. Where would Indian society go when there is injustice within the Mathas of Shankaracharyas? Currently, Hindu society is suffering from several problems and a very important problem is the caste system. Time and again, many of the seers, sages, social activists and philosophers have assailed this caste system. Politicians in any case keep assailing the same. But, politicians who assail it actually have their self-interest in their mind. Hence, when politicians talk of removing caste system, they intentionally turn the issue in a way that results in caste system getting stronger instead of getting weakened. The measures that are being proposed for eradication

Our current Shankaracharyas are not able to take any concrete steps for the remedy of these problems. They have more faith on conservatism in the name of tradition.

of caste related discriminations are not going to be effective. Rather, narrow economic, political and social self-interests are growing to maintain this caste system and these self-interests are just going on increasing. Even most of the important politicians of the country today are indirectly active to ensure that the roots of caste system continue to get stronger.

Until the Hindu society stops its caste-based discriminations and finds a solution to the problems arising from caste and sub caste systems, this society would not be able to offer anything to the world. The world would either call this society a sham or hypocritical, or believe that the leaders of this society are not credible. Some years back, during the Dharma convention held under the auspices of Vishva Hindu Parishad on the occasion of Kumbh, Shankaracharya of Kanchi Kamakoti Jayendra Saraswati had rightly pronounced that now development of Hindu culture was possible only through behaviour and not through preaching. It is in the aspect of behaviour that Hindus are being proven to be weakest and behaviour is the domain where our spiritual leaders are continuously failing. Spiritual leaders of the country talk about Dharma but do not talk about behaviour. They do not explain clearly the differences between Dharma and behaviour. There may be two reasons for the same. Firstly, very few of our spiritual leaders actually know the fundamental difference between Dharma and behaviour. Secondly, their own arrogance has made them so egotistic that they are finding themselves unable to encounter truth.

Firstly, very few of our spiritual leaders actually know the fundamental difference between Dharma and behaviour. Secondly, their own arrogance has made them so egotistic that they are finding themselves unable to encounter truth.

Dharma is in itself eternal. Every object has its Dharma. Everything that can be viewed or understood by our senses has its own separate Dharma. Stone has its Dharma, tree has its Dharma, the Sun has its Dharma - not only that, even pen and paper or every instrument being used in our day-to-day life definitely has some or other Dharma. The Dharma of an object or instrument or creature becomes the identity of its existence. If an object loses its Dharma, it loses its existence. Similarly, man has his Dharma and that Dharma only identifies him as man, else there is no difference between a man and an animal. This is an eternal truth that man also has his Dharma; however, as far as behaviour is concerned, it cannot be same for all and also it cannot be eternal. That means, behaviour would be always dynamic and the system of assigning behaviour would be formulated by spiritual leaders or powers based on place, time and circumstances. The behaviour and costume that are useful for a sizzling desert would not be applicable for the icy fields of Arctic, as such behaviour would result in the death of a person. Seers and maharishis of primeval India always provided dispensations for behaviour as per place, time and circumstances and called such dispensations 'Dharma' colloquially. However, when they used the word 'Dharma' in reference to behaviour, they knew that the form of Dharma was different from behaviour. The goal of behaviour is to further develop a society, to resolve the problems of society and to fill the society with more enthusiasm and jubilation. But, we cannot equate Dharma with behaviour. There would be differences between the two. Society also has its Dharma. It is the Dharma of a society to ensure that every person in the society is capable of developing himself as per his intellectual, rational and mental capacity and the society also continues to develop with development of its people. It is the Dharma of a society to ensure that the society does not fall into anarchy and every person continues to enjoy his rights. The core value of Dharma is duty-bound karma; this refers to those duty-bound karmas where no such thing should be done that we are not ready to accept if done to ourselves.

This is an eternal truth that man also has his Dharma; however, as far as behaviour is concerned,it cannot be same for all and also it cannot be eternal. That means,behaviour would be always dynamic.

It is expected from the current Shankaracharyas that they would explain to Indians and Hindus today what should be their ideals. This, considering the place, time and circumstances and what should be their duties in difference circumstances and which of the rules of society they should follow. However, it is unfortunate that neither Shankaracharyas nor 'Dharma Sansad', established by the Vishva Hindu Parishad many years back, are able to honestly mull over this issue. It is rather peculiar that they are accepting all the changes taking place on their own with passage of time but they are not ready to forcefully and honestly formulate any such dispensation that is capable of eradicating the evils of our society. Why is it like that? Let's take the example of our food habits and untouchability. Today, Hindus visit foreign countries and go to hotels and restaurants there. They do not question who had cooked their food. They also do not enquire about the castes of the cooks or ask if the vessels used for cooking were pure. They also do not enquire whether food was cooked with Ganges water or any other water. This is correct that spiritual gurus do not take non-vegetarian food and only eat vegetarian food and take fruits and milk. They do not bother, rather they cannot bother, to question who supplied the fruits and milk and who cultivated it, as the place, time and circumstances are compelling them to behave the way they are behaving. That very behaviour is also in accordance with Dharma. Dharma here does not refer to eternal Dharma of any specific object but to conventional behaviour that is also called duty-bound karma and when Hindus return from foreign countries they are not mocked in their Hindu society. They are able to mingle with their family and society and they do not need any purification, as was the practice some hundred years back. The vagaries of time have compelled Hindu spiritual gurus to accept foreign travels and eating habits of Hindus and disconnect the same from narrow interpretation of Dharma. Today, Shankaracharya or any spiritual guru does not care whether the chair that he is using in a plane was earlier used by a Sudra or a Brahmin or a Muslim or a Christian. Similarly, when he sits in a car, he does not enquire about the factory where the car was manufactured or about the persons who had used that seat before him. But, when the same Shankaracharya

> *It is expected from the current Shankaracharyas that they would explain to Indians and Hindus today what should be their ideals. This, considering the place, time and circumstances and what should be their duties.*

or spiritual guru visits the house of a devotee, the melodrama created by him is worth seeing. He demands that the place where he is supposed to sit must be cleaned with water from the Ganges and some specific cloth must be placed over the same and a throne must be arranged for him. Why create all this fuss? This hypocrisy would destroy Hindu society. Though this should be certainly ensured, considering that Shankaracharya is a spiritual guru of Hindu society, that the place where he is supposed to sit is neat and clean; but cleanliness does not mean that the place where he is supposed to sit should be purified with water from the Ganges.

I have seen the Pope caressing everybody. I have also seen this spiritual leader of Christians in pictures caressing African children and shaking hands with people without any discrimination. But, our Shankaracharyas do not do anything like that. I am not aware what they do with their staunch devotees, but they give even garlands and 'prasad' to other average people by throwing from a distance, just to ensure they do not touch them. Why is it so? The Shankaracharya of Kanchi Kamakoti has never been seen hugging a Harijan. Until our Shankaracharyas start hugging Harijans, it would be assumed that they do not have the respect towards Harijans that is essential in the current age. Hindu Dharma and Hindu culture do not differentiate between individuals. Why should there be any objection to hugging a hygienic person when the same Paramatma resides in everybody? When Shankaracharya can hug his staunch devotee, why can't he hug a Harijan? Listening to the problems of Harijans is a behaviour that is generally observed in common politicians of our country. The need of the day is to understand the feelings of Harijans, more than their problems. Hindus would have to now assimilate Harijans among themselves. It's not going to be enough to say that Harijans are our brothers. This would have to be demonstrated in action and this can happen only when the spiritual gurus of Hindus permit the same. The mistake that our spiritual gurus have committed

I have seen the Pope caressing everybody. I have also seen this spiritual leader of Christians in pictures caressing African children and shaking hands with people without any discrimination.

by formulating a system of caste by birth needs to be atoned. Blessed is Swami Dayananda Saraswati who established the Arya Samaj! He repeatedly said that caste should be determined by karma and not by birth. Blessed are those seers and sages who bashed the caste system! Even Bhagavan Buddha, Bhagavan Mahavira and all the greats of current age like Guru Nanakdevji Maharaj, Ravidas, Ramdas, Kabir, Swami Vivekananda and Maharishi Aurobindo saw a form of God in every human being. But it is regrettable that the current spiritual gurus refuse to accept the point of view of these godlike saints and mahatmas. Hindu society has still not been able to embrace the ideology of Vivekananda. Hindu society would not have undergone the kind of disintegration that is observed today if only it had accepted the process of assigning caste based on karma. Hindu society would be saved from this disintegration only when our Shankaracharyas and spiritual gurus take steps to eradicate caste-based discrimination in real sense. Today, Hindu society should successfully endeavour to eradicate its caste-based discrimination. Then only, this society would be able to provide such a leadership to the world that would be unprecedented. India would thus, not only be a frontrunner but would also become a real leader of the world. In fact, it is in the interest of the nation, the interest of Hindus and in the interest of mankind that the caste-based discrimination in Hindus is brought to an end. Would the real Shankaracharyas of Hindus do something for this? The four Mathas established by Adi Shankara should actually rekindle such a flame that is capable of eradicating caste-based discrimination once for all.

> *Blessed are those seers and sages who bashed the caste system! Even Bhagavan Buddha, Bhagavan Mahavira and all the greats of current age like Guru Nanakdevji Maharaj, Ravidas, Ramdas, Kabir and Swami Vivekananda.*

□□□